IS THE WORLD GROWING BETTER;

OR,

IS THE WORLD GROWING WORSE?

by

Henry Clay Morrison

First Fruits Press
Wilmore, Kentucky
c2013

ISBN: 9781621711094

Is the World Growing Better; or, Is the World Growing Worse? By Henry Clay Morrison
First Fruits Press, © 2013
Pentecostal Publishing Company, ©1932

Digital version at
http://place.asburyseminary.edu/firstfruitsheritagematerial/22/

First Fruits Press is a digital imprint of the Asbury Theological Seminary, B.L. Fisher Library. Asbury Theological Seminary is the legal owner of the material previously published by the Pentecostal Publishing Co. and reserves the right to release new editions of this material as well as new material produced by Asbury Theological Seminary. Its publications are available for noncommercial and educational uses, such as research, teaching and private study. First Fruits Press has licensed the digital version of this work under the Creative Commons Attribution Noncommercial 3.0 United States License. To view a copy of this license, visit http://creativecommons.org/licenses/by-nc/3.0/us/.

For all other uses, contact:

First Fruits Press
B.L. Fisher Library
Asbury Theological Seminary
204 N. Lexington Ave.
Wilmore, KY 40390
http://place.asburyseminary.edu/firstfruits

Morrison, H. C. (Henry Clay), 1857-1942.
   Is the world growing better; or, is the world growing worse? / by Henry Clay Morrison.
   172 p. ; 21 cm.
   Wilmore, Ky. : First Fruits Press, c2013.
   Reprint. Previously published: Wilmore, Ky. : Pentecostal Publishing Company, c1932.
   ISBN: 9781621711094 (pbk.)
   1. Methodist Church – Sermons. 2. Church and the world. 3. United States – Moral conditions. 4. United States – Social conditions. I. Title.
BX8333.M6 I8 2013   236.3

Cover design by Jane Brannen

asburyseminary.edu
800.2ASBURY
204 North Lexington Avenue
Wilmore, Kentucky 40390

Is The World Growing Better;

or,

Is The World Growing Worse?

By

Rev. HENRY CLAY MORRISON, D. D.

Author of: Sermons for the Times; The Christ of the Gospels; The Optimism of Premillennialism; World Tour of Evangelism; Second Coming of Christ; Romanism and Ruin; The Story of Two Lawyers; Remarkable Conversions; Prophecies Fulfilled and Fulfilling, and a number of Booklets.

1,000 printed April 1, 1932
1,000 printed Oct. 1, 1932

Pentecostal Publishing Company, Incorporated,
Louisville, Kentucky.

COPYRIGHT, 1932,

BY

THE PENTECOSTAL PUBLISHING COMPANY,

LOUISVILLE, KENTUCKY.

DEDICATION

This volume is humbly dedicated to all those children of God who believe that, as the dark hour precedes the dawning of the day, the untoward conditions existing in the world at this time are the forerunners of the coming of a glorious day when men shall learn war no more, and Jesus Christ shall reign triumphantly, and the prophecy in the angelic song which welcomed his birth shall be fulfilled with "Glory to God in the highest; and on earth, peace, good will toward men."

PREFACE

I never like a lengthy preface to a book. The only way to find out the contents of a volume is to read it. The chapters herein contained have thrust themselves into my mind as I have read and traveled and thought on existing world conditions.

There is a kind of optimism among men that arises out of an eagerness for what they call "progress." In times of peace and supposed prosperity men largely ignore facts as they really exist. We by no means shut our eyes to the good that is in the world, but in this volume we are thinking and writing of the tremendous drift toward evil, and what we believe means a crisis in world history. We confine our observations, however, largely to these United States.

There is a strange portend in the atmosphere, a kind of suspense. Philosophers and statesmen hardly dare to prognosticate what the near future holds. There is a very general conviction among thoughtful people that present conditions cannot exist for long; there must be a turning back to practical living, to economy, to the fear of God and an altruistic attitude toward mankind, or a fearful crash of modern civilization. H. C. MORRISON.

CONTENTS

1. The Ebb and Flow of History ... 9
2. The Brighter Side of History 19
3. An Age of Invention 27
4. The Financial Feature of the Machine Age 41
5. The Old Political Parties 49
6. The Menace of the Millionaires .. 61
7. Does the Present Outlook Promise World Peace? 70
8. Our Young People are Not Being Taught Religion in the Schools .. 83
9. What Our Young People are Being Taught in the Schools 91
10. The Harvest 103
11. Trying to Get Rid of God 113
12. The General Drift 127
13. Ecclesiasticism Versus Evangelism 144
14. Are We Approaching the End of the Age? 160

CHAPTER I.

THE EBB AND FLOW OF HISTORY

Is the world growing better; or, is the world growing worse? is an old and oft-repeated question. Anything like a correct and satisfactory answer is difficult. The question embraces a vast territory and thousands of years of time. It covers not only all nations but all history. It would take a person of very wide and accurate knowledge of the past and present conditions of different nationalities, tribes, and peoples of the earth, with a careful study of a vast background of history, to give an answer to this old question that would be considered with any degree of satisfaction or assurance that the answer was approximately correct.

This writer makes no claim to have a wide knowledge of the different peoples of the earth or anything approaching an accurate conception of human history. With such knowledge as we possess, we can but think, and we are here putting down some of our thoughts, that they may suggest deeper, wider, and more correct thought on the part of those who may read the contents of this book.

Human history has been something like a vast ocean with its flow and ebb. There have been periods of high tide in progress, development, and great advancement in civilization, the uplift and betterment of the peoples of some of the great nations of the world. Again, there have been fearful ebb-tides when selfishness seemed to have leadership and control of men, when human hatred broke out into devastating flames of war; men were slain in the morning of life by millions. The aftermath of these wars which left poverty, confusion, and burdens of taxes which bowed the backs of the people, seemed to block every avenue of advancement. Plagues broke out. Disease spread its black wing over vast regions of country. The largest and most prosperous cities became charnel houses of death and desolation. Those who were spared from sword and fire and plague stood desolate and amazed at the ruin which surrounded them and evidently believed and, would have said without hesitation, "The world is

Is the World Growing Worse? 11

growing worse. The human race is marching toward certain doom."

Eventually the tide turns. The flow of industry, prosperity, and progress has come rolling in to higher levels of freedom and a more advanced and hopeful civilization than had been known before. Times of peace have always been times for the betterment of social conditions. The learned have had opportunity to teach the ignorant. There has been the dissemination of better ideals of life, and hopes for a peaceful, contented and progressive world have comforted the hearts of thinking and humane men.

Egypt once had a great civilization; the magnificence of her ruins tells of her splendor in the day of her wealth and power. Her glory faded, and her power passed away.

Under the rulership of Nebuchadnezzar Babylon became a great city, the center and glory of pagan civilization. She was Queen of the Orient. Trade and wealth flowed into her like rivers flow to the sea. She had the appearance of being impregnable to any and all outside foes, but in her wealth and luxury she became wicked, blasphemous, and so depraved that her sin called for fearful judgment. Babylon fell. The place where she once stood in splendor and pride became a desolation. The ebb-tide so receded that along the shores of time there was naught to be seen of this powerful center of wealth and progress but the wreckage and ruin of that which promised to be permanent and abiding through the ages wielding influences that would have had a beneficent effect upon mankind.

Nineveh was a great city with marts of trade, palaces of wealth, with her teeming thousands of human beings, but she fell, and the sands of time and the dust of the centuries have so buried her glory that it is with difficulty that archeologists locate the spot where she once stood.

The Greeks reached a remarkable state of civilization. Under the Greeks, architecture and art reached a height of power and beauty which has not been surpassed. But Athens came finally to her climax of greatness. Decay set in and her splendid ruins stand as a warning to men that they but build for decay; that the feet of ruin march

Is the World Growing Worse? 13

rapidly behind what is supposed to be permanent; that men who do not believe in, reverence, and obey God, with their proudest achievements, are doomed to perish, and that by and by all their splendid works leave nothing behind but a sad testimony that man in himself is a failure and that which he builds upon a mere foundation of his own wisdom and ambition is destined to fall.

Rome became the mistress of the world. She was a center of commerce and wealth. Her literature, art, and eloquence reached a remarkable height of perfection and beauty. She majored on law. Roman kings, consuls, and armies became the rulers of almost the entire world. One is impressed with their high ideals of justice. Under the Roman sceptre conditions of peace were brought to all the greater nations and almost the entire world. Good roads were built. There was much travel. There was large traffic by sea. Many of the comforts and luxuries of an advanced civilization were enjoyed. Human progress seemed to be at floodtide, but the ebb came and Rome fell.

There was a time when it seemed as if Palestine would become the center of a civilization that would bless the world. David conquered the enemies of Israel. Solomon, his son, took the throne at a time of great peace and Jerusalem became one of the most beautiful cities and attractive centers in all the world. The magnificence of the temple built by Solomon, with his own palace, attracted the attention and admiration of pagan potentates of many countries. It looked as if Jerusalem would grow in wealth, power and population until the hills and valleys surrounding the sacred city would be laid out in streets and built up with marts of trade and palaces of splendor. There was every indication that Jerusalem would abide a joy in the earth. But sin came and rose into a flood of wickedness. Jerusalem fell. Her streets ran red with blood and billows of fire swept away the glory of the temple, the palaces, and everything that had promised to abide and bless humanity.

No one can read ancient history without being impressed with the fact that there were **periodically** high tides of prosperity

Is the World Growing Worse? 15

and promise followed by ebb-tides of war which left destruction and ruin in its trail. And so it has been in modern history. It is not worth while to go into details. Think for a moment of the Thirty Years' War in Europe with its toll of death, devastation, poverty, and general paralysis of all hope for progress, of all those things that count largest in the peace and happiness of the people. In more modern times we had the Reign of Terror in France. Then came the Napoleon wars, deluging Europe with blood and sweeping it with fire. Then the Franco-Prussian War. It would take a large volume to write any sort of history of the wars of the British Isles both among themselves and with foreign countries. The history of these United States is a history of war and recuperation and renewed preparation for engagement in more war.

This writer has lived to see the ravages of a civil war; several wars on the western front with the Indians, not so destructive to our government, but fearfully hard on the Indians; then the war with Spain; then came the war with the Philippine Islands; then the Boxer War with China. The war between China and Japan made a slaughter-pen of China. For years battlefields were white with the bones of Chinamen slain in that war who were never buried. The war between Russia and Japan was a fearful tragedy of blood and death. The history of Mexico and South America has been one succession of tyrannical rule, revolution, war, death, poverty, ignorance, dirt, and bloody rags.

Three decades ago there was a general feeling that a new era of peace had dawned upon the world, that men had outgrown their thirst for blood, that nations had advanced to a stage of civilization when their rulers could sit down, discuss their differences with wisdom and the spirit of fraternity and peace. Eloquent orators on the chautauqua platforms were telling us that the captains of industry would not permit wars to break out among the nations. They told us that the shuttle of commerce flying to and fro in the peaceful warp of international life would make war impossible. They assured us that the great labor unions of the world had cultivated a fraternal spirit of genuine brotherhood that would

Is the World Growing Worse? 17

make it impossible for them to lay down the tools of toil and take up the arms of destruction. They also assured us that the implements of warfare had been so improved that no army could last longer than for a few conflicts. They glorified science which had developed the instruments of death up to a point when men would not dare to employ them in battle against each other. They also said that explosives had not only become so destructive that it would be inhuman to use them, but they were so expensive that in one battle a nation would shoot away all of its financial resources. The great crowds at the chautauquas cheered and waved their handkerchiefs as they listened with delight to these eloquent prophets of peace. But while the orators entertained the people, the war clouds were gathering, and in a fatal moment an assassination was committed that started the roll of the war drums, and set echoing through the earth the blast of the military bugle that summoned millions of young men to one of the most titanic and destructive struggles in all the history of the world.

Finally, when the firing ceased and the

rulers of the nations sat down at the council table to build a tower of peace, it turned out that there was a confusion of tongues and they entered into covenants, slicing up the nations, shipping vast populations from one place to another and laying the dry kindling wood of hatred ready for fires of strife and jealousy that it seems almost certain at some time, perhaps in the not distant future, will break out in a more devastating flame of fire and bloodshed than the world has ever known.

As one broods over the tragedies of the past and the present condition of confusion, and mistrust he asks himself the oft-repeated question, Is the world growing better; or, is the world growing worse?

CHAPTER II.

THE BRIGHTER SIDE OF HISTORY.

Up out of the conflict of the centuries, in spite of all the ebb-tides of time, there has come larger liberty and a better civilization. Many of the wars of the past have been fought for the overthrow of tyrannical rulership and the freedom and better economic and social conditions of mankind.

Great pity these benefits could not have come without bloodshed, but it seems that men are so selfish and stupid that the shackles of slavery must sometimes be broken with the hammer of Mars. Out of the French Revolution there came a better France. Out of the revolution led by Cromwell came a better England. Out of the American Revolution came the United States, and out of the Civil War came the freedom of six millions of slaves and a far better condition for the masters of those slaves. Along a bloody pathway has come a better Mexico. Under the domination of British rule, notwithstanding the heavy yoke and the discontent, there has come a better India. And thus humanity in the midst of blood and fire has fought its way onward and upward. To be sure, it is unfortunate that men have found it necessary to climb to higher heights of civilization over the dead bodies of the foes of all progress, but there have always been heroes who will fight and, if need be, die for high ideals, the largest freedom for themselves and their fellow-beings.

Dr. Livingstone blazed a trail of light through darkest Africa. He has been followed by many faithful souls and, notwithstanding the difficulties with which religion and civilization have had to contend, many people in the Dark Continent have come to sit clothed and in their right minds at the feet of the world's Redeemer; in many places the light which promises a better day is breaking in upon Africa. The story of the suffering of those black people, their mistreatment, the enslavement of hundreds of thousands, the cruel butchery in which white men have been involved, is heartbreaking, but there has been much abatement of this cruelty and out of the darkness come many of these backward people singing a song of joy and hope.

Is the World Growing Worse? 21

For many years chaos and war have ravaged China, but in spite of it all there are indications of an awakening to better things in that vast nation. The Chinese are a powerful people physically, mentally, and industrially. If they could be Christianized they would make a tremendous contribution to the genuine progress of the world. If they become schooled in war and well trained in modern science and learn how to use the fearful forces of destruction without the Christian faith they will certainly be a menace to civilization.

In the remote regions of the earth there is an intellectual quickening. Mission stations are planted, schools are opened, hospitals are built, and the Gospel of Jesus Christ is being proclaimed. Much is taking place in the dark places of the earth to encourage earnest effort and holy enthusiasm on the part of those who love humanity and trust in God and seek to bring light and health to those who sit in the darkness of ignorance and superstition.

In many of the remote and benighted parts of the world the Gospel of Jesus Christ is proving its power to save from the uttermost of human degradation and is making saints of the vilest of human beings. As never before in history, the rulers and representatives of the people are striving to bring about the end of war and the promotion of peace and good will among men. It is quite certain if any one of the great nations of the earth should make war upon any other nation for purposes of conquest, such nation would meet with almost universal censure and protest from the more advanced and civilized nations of the world. We might go forward enumerating much that is hopeful for a better world in the way of aggressive forces of education, of efforts to decrease illiteracy, the splendid work of the Red Cross in alleviating human suffering, the community chests of our great cities which distribute hundreds of thousands, yes, millions of dollars, among those who are pressed with want. As never before orphanages are being built, homes for the aged, hospitals for the sick, and various institutions for the help of delinquent and suffering people.

All of this good work is a testimony to the influence of the religion of Jesus Christ among men. Contemplating these many indications of improvement of conditions, enlargement of sympathy and charity, one is encouraged to hope for better conditions.

Medical science has made remarkable progress. The prevalence of the great contagious plagues which once swept helpless millions into death, almost unhindered, has now been so mastered that they are quite unknown, as they once existed. Yellow fever, cholera, and other plagues which at one time seemed to have the mastery of men, have been arrested and, among more civilized people, have almost disappeared. We must not forget, however, in our optimistic moments that, a few years ago, a strange disease, called influenza, before which medical science stood appalled, swept its millions from the earth.

Some of the best trained medical minds, with a strong inclination to pessimism, will tell you that the fearful plague of other years took away the weaker and unfit units of society and left the stronger and better to propagate the race, and now, that these plagues having disappeared, the weaker members of the race are reproducing the species, and that there is danger of a very general breakdown of both the physical and intellectual powers of mankind. They will tell you that cancer, diabetes and the tendency toward tubercular troubles are greatly on the increase. Let us hope for the better, rather than prophesy the worst.

There are, however, some very serious questions which thrust themselves upon us that must not be overlooked. If you should put this question, Is the World Growing Better? to leading educators, politicians, men of business, men of the scientific world, and the prominent men of the various ecclesiasticisms, you would no doubt, get a diversity of replies; but most of them would tell you that this is a progressive age, that the world is growing better. They would be thinking of the general advancement of scientific discovery, of education, of travel, commerce, rapid transportation and the accumulation of wealth. So far as these things are concerned, no doubt there is progress; but we are thinking and writing from an entirely different viewpoint.

Let us put the question this way: Are men becoming more honest and pure in life?

Is the World Growing Worse? 25

Are women becoming more modest and chaste in character and conduct? Are marriage vows kept with greater sacredness? Are bankers and those you have trusted with the safe keeping and investment of money more trustworthy? Are children more obedient, industrious, economical and helpful in family life? Is the family more compact, orderly, and are all of its ties more sacred? Are the preachers of the gospel more devout, faithful to the word of God, and zealous in the proclamation of the gospel? Are church-members more spiritual, self-sacrificing and consecrated to God's service? Are the worldly masses outside of the church more ready to hear and respond to the gospel message? In fact, is the general trend of things in all of these realms of human society better than in the past?

In seeking a definition to the word "progress," one must consider many phases of human life. Perhaps, the word "progress" has been a bit overworked the last few decades. The optimistic orator is wont to reach a climax with the statement that "these United States have developed the most progressive civilization in the history of the world." Thoughtful people are beginning to place a question mark at the end of this oratorical flourish.

There must be a very distinct line drawn between material and spiritual progress. There may be discoveries that lead to the physical benefit of mankind. Wealth may increase, luxuries and pleasures which wealth brings, may overflow the banks of reason and the dykes of sober caution, and, like Mississippi floods, devastate all surrounding plantations, inundate and sweep away moral and spiritual barriers to the irreparable hurt of the higher life of the nation.

Unfortunately, our American people have come to look upon wealth almost as a virtue. You would think from the passionate pursuit of money and material things, that our Lord Jesus has said, How hardly shall a poor man enter into the Kingdom of Heaven? when, in fact, he said, "How hardly shall a rich man enter into the Kingdom of Heaven?"

We leave the thoughts expressed in this chapter for the consideration and sober judgment of a jury made up of our readers.

CHAPTER III.

AN AGE OF INVENTION.

We are living in an age of discovery and invention. Some of the greatest inventions in all history have been made in the last hundred years. The telegraph, steamboat, railway trains, have all come into popular use within the comparatively short space of a century. There is a sense in which these inventions have largely extended, if not a man's life, his opportunities. When men traversed the seas in sailing ships, they often spent many months in crossing the Atlantic, which can now be accomplished in a few days. Travel on horseback, or oxcart over mud roads was with labor and difficulty, and consumed much time out of the short years of a man's life. There is no way to estimate the advantages of communication by telegraph, steamships and railway trains.

The telephone, the phonograph, the moving picture, the radio, the automobile, the airship, the undersea boat, the X-ray and, many other inventions I might mention, have come into existence since this writer was born. You can hardly begin the construction of a building of any importance that the architects and contractors will not come to you with some new invention to be used in the building of the edifice of decided advantage in its strength, utility and beauty. One of the most important inventions of modern times, as a labor saving machine, is the linotype, and along with this goes the typewriter. The list of inventions, if named, would be almost innumerable. They have been of a character to relieve the housewife of much drudgery, and have lifted many heavy burdens from the back of the farmer. Volumes might be written on discoveries and inventions in every branch of science that have made their contributions to the convenience and comfort of mankind.

Sad to say, much inventive genius has been devoted to the discovery and invention of methods and machinery for the wholesale slaughter of humanity. The long range cannon, the rapid-fire gun, poison gas, explosives dropped from airships, and ingenious and diabolical means for the distribution of disease germs, have all come into use within the past few decades. The tremendous destructive power of various explosives is a menace to life and property in the hands of vicious men, fearful to contemplate.

The moving picture is one of the most remarkable inventions of modern times. It has been seized upon by heartless greed and, while quite interesting, has been largely turned into a demoralizing school of vice for the kindling of the most dangerous passions of which human beings are capable. We shall not go into any general discussion of the vile use of the moving picture, but will quote a part of an article which recently appeared in The Alabama Christian Advocate, from Bishop Warren A. Candler, one of the most thoughtful and clear-minded Christian philosophers of our time:

"Bishop George Horne of Norwich, author of a celebrated 'Commentary on the Psalms,' said, 'It is well known what strange work there has been in the world, under the name and pretence of reformation; how often it has turned out to be in reality deformation.'

"This wise and witty observation applies with great force to the frequent promises of Mr. Will Hayes for the reformation of the 'Movies.'

"When Mr. Hayes was first employed by the owners and operators of those vice-laden shows, it was given out that his chief function was to be that of reforming them—an absurd announcement that the movie people were so eager to reform their demoralizing exhibitions that they would pay a man $100,000 a year to cleanse them and keep them clean.

"Now Mr. Hayes comes forward, after all these years, with a new promise of reformation to take effect next year. This is a confession that they are bad now, and will continue their badness for another six months, and then become good. Thus Mr. Hayes makes a New Year resolution on their behalf six months in advance.

"Upon this almost laughable promise the Christian Century comments as follows:

"Mr. Will Hayes announces that next year's movies are to be much cleaner. Crime and sex are to fade out —or at least be dimmed. Confirming his promise in their usual way, his employers have also announced what they expect to present to our children. Fox films, for example, will give them a long list. Among the titles and descriptions are the following: 'Bad Girl —red-lipped shop-girl. . . . wanted things, clothes, boy friends, kisses. Aching with suppressed emotions.' 'The Yellow Ticket—modest maid, chaste, lovely—caught in the avid clutch of ignoble nobles—lured to luxury, branded by the sign of shame.' 'Wicked—Gun moll with a baby. Was she wicked or weak' 'The Hysterical Age. . . . whoopee-making on the primrose path where only primroses are prim. Kiss-as-kiss-can comedy. . . . pettying and partying.' 'In Her Arms,' 'Sugar Daddies,' 'Devil's Daughter,' 'Champangne,' 'Alimony

Queens,' and several more of the same kind. Universal, not to be outdone, announces that among its 1932 pictures will be these: 'Baby-Faced Gangster,' 'Bullet Proof,' 'Homicide Squad,' 'Derailed,' the latter about 'men hard as nails and women who want to be taken.' Also, 'Waterloo Bridge—in spite of her lurid past, in spite of her scarlet present, he loved her.' Paramount announces a similar offering of old sewage in new pipes and promises this contribution to international good will: 'Daughter of the Dragon—a tingling thriller of a beautiful Chinese girl used to entrap men.' (Wait until this reaches China!) Well, which has faded out—crime and sex filth or Mr. Hayes' promise?"

"The reformation of theatrical performances, in all their manifold exhibitions, has been promised many, many times for centuries past,—since 'the memory of man runneth not back to the contrary,' as the lawyers say. But the reformation has never come to pass.

"The poet Pollock said of it:

" 'The theatre from the first
Was the favorite haunt of sin,
Though honest men—some very honest, wise and
worthy men—
Thought it might be turned to good account;
And so perhaps it might, but never was;
From first to last it was an evil place.' "

Is it not correct, when we come to weigh the invention of the moving picture in the balance of reason, that we conclude that it has not only been a real moral disadvantage, but also a financial detriment? It has drained untold millions of money from the common people to fill the coffers of a very few persons with countless millions of money. Meanwhile, these few persons, living selfishly in imagined enjoyment of their wealth, appear to be absolutely indifferent to the moral blight they are bringing upon the nation.

The automobile is a remarkable invention. It enables people to travel with great rapidity and comfort, and if properly used, no doubt could make a substantial contribution to the welfare of mankind. But whether it has been a valuable asset, is a question a bit difficult to answer. Automobile accidents in this country in 1931 caused the deaths of 34,400 persons and non-fatal injuries to nearly a million more. This death and injury toll equals the combined population of Nevada, Delaware, Wyoming and the national capital.

The population of each of fifteen states was less than the number of persons killed and injured and only five largest American cities had populations in 1930 greater than the 1931 automobile accident total.

The economic loss due to these accidents is estimated at two and one-half billion dollars. This is more than the cost of public school education in the United States; five times the country's average yearly fire loss; and more than half the amount required to maintain all the agencies of the federal government each year.

These are comparisons that drive home the realization of a tragic condition. If we had not reached a state of mind when we appear to care but little for human life, a tremendous storm of protest would be raised against the careless operation of automobiles. The invention and use of this modern convenience have not only been fearfully destructive to human life, but it has impoverished millions of people. They have invested their money in cars instead of homes; many of them have been rushing to and fro to the neglect of sober living and remunerative industry. Hundreds of thousands have mortgaged their homes to buy cars; in short time, a few years at most, the cars become junk with the mortgages unpaid. Many people keep their cars for a year, perhaps, which has been bought with borrowed money, then exchange them for new, or better cars, before the first car is paid for, thus plunging deeper and deeper into debt.

The automobile has proven a great asset to the lawless. It comes next to firearms with robbers of every kind. In thousands of instances its rapid movement has enabled robbers and murderers to make their getaway from the officers of the law. The most degrading, well-dressed scoundrel in any town or village can call up a modest, unsuspecting girl in a Christian home, meet her down street in his automobile, whisk her away to a roadhouse, have dinner, with some dope, and return her within a block of her home; she can saunter in as demure as if she had been down-town to price a pair of shoes. There is no way to calculate the moral degradation that has come to many young people of this nation through the automobile which has furnished opportunity to evade observation, to trail up quiet country roads and park, with lights turned out. A distinguished United States senator not long since, speaking of some of the very serious conditions in the social life of the nation, said, "many automobiles were simply a red-light district on wheels."

I read not long since from a reliable source, that the twenty-six million of automobiles in this country had cost the people five billions, four hundred and sixty millions, seven hundred and sixteen thousand, six hundred and twenty dollars, He went on to say that the country owned so many automobiles, at such tremendous cost, that we hardly knew how to get through the winter without starving. We hardly think any one will insist that the automobile has made any contribution to the spiritual life or the moral uplift of the American people. Of course, it has come to stay, and can be utilized to great conven-

Is the World Growing Worse? 37

ience and comfort; but we find that any invention can become a menace to the welfare of a people when it is seized upon by wicked and reckless hands. The expenditure of the vast sum of money mentioned above must be repeated every few years.

The Radio is one of the wonders of the world; one of the most startling triumphs of modern science, but in the wrong hands, and under immoral influences, it can pour a stream of trash, foolishness and propaganda of every kind, which is not conducive to high ideals and genuine spiritual development into the homes of the people. The Radio is bringing to people teachings by skeptical preachers that will undermine evangelical Christian faith and prove a wide sowing of tares of unbelief that will be disastrous to spiritual life and upright conduct.

I am not writing against scientific discoveries. I offer no objection to scientific investigation, or modern inventions of any kind, but I am asking the question of serious thinking people, have these inventions lifted up high moral standards, or contributed to the deepening of the spiritual life of the nation? Has our world become a better world, because of these inventions? Those things that might be a large contribution to the usefulness and happiness of mankind, in the hands of selfish and wicked people, may become most destructive. We may boast of the airship, but what a fearful instrument of death, desolation and actual destruction, not only of all progress, but of the race itself, in case of war. All things fail if man fails to fear God and keep his commandments.

We quote here a clipping from *The St. Louis Christian Advocate*, some profoundly suggestive statements, by Mr. Roger Babson, one of the leading business men of the nation:

> "Churches have a great opportunity, for man has a spiritual side as well as a physical or intellectual. They are far more necessary to an efficient community than the dispensary or schools, and preachers are needed by the people much more than are physicians or college professors.
>
> "What are the fundamental teach-

ings of Jesus? Briefly Jesus taught that men and women fail to live truly, and really amount to nothing unless they have spirituality. The spiritual force underlies everything and without it nothing worth while can be accomplished. The old religions gave the letter of the law, but it remained for Jesus to emphasize the spirit of the law. Yet, spiritual needs can be met only by spiritual means. Governmental laws, methods and organizations are of no value unless men and women are filled with truth, righteousness and mercy. Material things have no power to raise the sunken spirit. Gravitation, electricity and steam are great forces, but they are all powerless to change the motives of men and women. The wealth of a Rockefeller cannot heal a broken heart and the wisdom of all our universities cannot turn into the paths of righteousness a wayward soul. Men can be born again only through religion. To make men over is the real purpose and function of the churches.

"The churches have the only solution to the problems of today. The future of America and the entire world is bound up with the future of the churches."

Is the church performing her proper function? Is the world coming under the power of the Church, or is the Church becoming more worldly? Are there any clear lines of demarcation drawn today between those of the world, and those of the Church?

CHAPTER IV.

THE FINANCIAL FEATURE OF THE MACHINE AGE.

In the preceding chapter we had something to say with reference to the effect of the automobile on the moral and spiritual life of the people. We hardly think there is any one who will contend that the automobile, however swiftly it may travel, and the fact that we have enough of them in this country to haul our hundred and fifty millions of people at one time, that this attractive vehicle is bringing us to a higher plane of moral and spiritual life.

Of course all readers will understand that we would not, for a moment, indicate that the automobile is not a remarkable invention. It has led to the construction of good roads, easy and rapid travel. Many people have taken advantage of these facts who were somewhat shut up in their home community and have toured the country, visited historic places, and have doubtless enlarged their intellectual and social life; but the subject under consideration is, the spiritual life of the people, that life of deepest and highest meaning which makes largest contribution to the building of character, and putting into the national life those elements that make for genuine progress and assurance of peace and prosperity which secure the well being of all the people of our great nation.

The question which we now raise, Has the automobile proven an economic asset? Has it been a financial benefit to the people at large? It certainly has not. It has been the means of the accumulation of vast fortunes for the few. It has furnished employment at living wages for a large number of people; at the same time, is it not a fact, or at least quite probable, that it has impoverished millions of people, and had much to do with the present nation-wide depression.

It is well known that the automobile has made multi-millionaires of a few men —Raskob, Ford, and others who might be mentioned. At the same time, hundreds of thousands in these United States have mortgaged their homes, in many instances their household furniture, in order to pur-

Is the World Growing Worse? 43

chase automobiles. It seems that the car gliding swiftly over smooth roads creates a sort of reckless disposition to spend money freely. A man with a mortgaged home for a fine automobile pulls up to a filling station and hands out his money as if he were a rich banker, or receiving an immense income from a skyscraper which he owns without any mortgage attachments.

Mother Earth furnishes us with our living; our food and clothing come from her generous bosom. We clothe ourselves with the wool, the cotton, the linen, the silks, in fact, everything we wear is given to us by the generous hand of Mother Earth. The cereals, the nuts, the fruits, the vegetables and the animals upon which we subsist all come from Mother Earth. If the earth fails because of drouth or other reasons to yield her increase, there is suffering, famine, death; when the earth pours forth her abundance want disappears and there is health and happiness.

The farmer, the tiller of the soil, that element of society that brings forth out of the earth the fundamental supplies of human life, forms the most important factor in human society. When the farmer prospers all trades and business prosper. When the farmer fails all branches of business, in the nature of things, must suffer. If rain ceases to fall the springs cannot run, the streams cease to flow, river beds are dry; the boats of traffic are tied up, weeds grow between the cross-ties of the railroad, and commerce comes to a standstill; gaunt want is abroad in the land, unrest, revolution, blood and fire. The farmer is to the whole of our commercial life what rain is to the springs and streams that make the rivers that carry the commerce.

In the present depression the farmer is the great sufferer. His problems, it seems, cannot be solved. He cannot sow his seed or plow his furrows with hope; his products accumulate upon his hands; the earth brings forth abundantly, but he finds no market for his surplus, the result is, he has no money to deposit in his town bank, and the bank closes. He has nothing with which to purchase products of the factory and the factory closes. Merchants make assignment, bankruptcy spreads on every hand and millions of idle workers are searching in

Is the World Growing Worse? 45

vain for a job, after awhile they become hungry, their families are suffering, they become desperate; finding nothing to eat, and no employment for their willing hands, they become thirsty for blood; the tools of toil refusing to yield them a competency, they seize upon the implements of destruction. The implements of destruction can never produce an abundant supply for the needs of men, they can never bring peace and plenty and contentment.

Is there no remedy for the present depressed condition in these United States? Yes, there is a remedy, but the people will never consent for its application. Suppose some friendly genie at the setting of the sun could wave a magic wand over the nation that would destroy every gasoline propelled vehicle of travel, or road and farm machinery; suppose this same genie at the rising of the sun could wave this same magic wand over the nation and bring into existence fifty millions of good strong horses, what a transformation that would be! One splendid result—the people would stay at home for awhile and get acquainted with each other. At once harness makers would be compelled to employ two millions of men to make harness for these horses; those building and keeping roads in order would need to employ a million men to take the place of road machinery; the wagon, buggy and carriage factories would call for three or four millions of men to build vehicles.

These fifty millions of horses would eat a hundred millions of bushels of corn in less than a month; within one week, after they appeared on the scene, wheat would shoot up to $1.50 and $2.00 per bushel. All farm products—corn, wheat, oats, hay—and everything that grows upon the farm would be valuable; the millions of the capitalists would begin to flow back to farm populations, the town bank would be prosperous, the thrifty farmers would flock to the stores to supply their needs, the factories would be compelled to put on a full force of laborers and work day and night to supply the demands of prosperous people. There would be a call for farm labor at good wages; there would not be an idle man in the nation, who was willing to work. It would become necessary for Congress to widen the doors of immigration that the demand for

Is the World Growing Worse? 47

labor in this country could be supplied. The demand for horses would be urgent; the half of this fifty million horses would produce colts. Figure out $50.00 per head for twenty-five million colts every year, for ten years, and then on and on, and you will find hundreds of millions of dollars flowing into the pockets of the farmer. There will be no need for a farm board or a government bank taking mortgages on farms.

We understand that there are two sides to every proposition. Some one can easily argue that doing away with the automobile would put a vast number out of employment, but we can safely answer that would be a trifle compared to the tremendous demand that would accrue from labor, should horse power be substituted for gasoline power. Some one may insist that cattle, sheep, chickens and hogs can consume the products of the farm, but the fact is, they do not do so. The farmer hauls his products to town, sells what he can for almost nothing, often for less than it costs to produce same, and returns home heartsick with the products of his labor for which he finds no market.

Of course, we understand that the genie with the wonder-working wand will not appear; and the automobile, with its reckless drivers, will continue its history of rapid movement, leaving its thirty-four thousand dead every twelve months in its trail, with its one million cripples, many of them for life. A relentless war will continue to be waged against humanity. We have not written this chapter with any thought that it will bring the changes suggested, but people are constantly asking with befuddled brains and mystified looks, What's the matter with the country? What has brought about present conditions? The thoughts expressed here will be at least, a partial answer to this question which is being asked by distressed millions of American people.

What we call progress can move so rapidly that no steering gear can control its movement and hold it on the track of National safety.

CHAPTER V.

THE OLD POLITICAL PARTIES.

Since the close of the Civil War the government of this republic has been under the control of two great political parties. Whatever may be thought or said of these parties, under their direction and guidance the land has had a prosperity and development never equalled, perhaps, in the history of the world, and the people have enjoyed a protection and liberty as nearly ideal, as has ever existed among men.

The territory under our flag is large, with varied climates, enterprises and interests, sometimes supposed to be conflicting, which, at times, has produced sectional prejudices which have been unfortunate; but in times of distress or war, all lines of demarcation have disappeared and the nation has been one vast united people, standing together with high resolves, noble and humane ideals.

While the Republican party has held the reins of government most of the time, the Democratic party has been a powerful influence in the balancing of justice. Each great party has been a checkmate on the other, so that, on the whole, we have had most excellent government. Unfortunately, at the present, there are indications of disruption, and the breaking up of the old parties at a time when there is much unrest and dissatisfaction among large groups of our people. The disintegration of either, or both, of the old parties would give opportunity for the organization of a strong radical party, under the leadership of a very dangerous class of men with convictions and objectives quite out of harmony with those principles that have dominated and guided our American life and civilization.

The disagreements and antagonisms that break up the harmony in the Republican party seem to arise out of the fact that the East is a manufacturing and mining country which insists on a high protective tariff, while the West is largely an agricultural and stock raising section, and would prefer a lower tariff. Then, the East wants a low, or no, tariff on petroleum shipped from South America, in order that it may have cheap fuel; while the West is a great

Is the World Growing Worse? 51

petroleum region and wants protection of its oil output.

There are other conflicting opinions and interests in this wide stretch of country from the Atlantic to the Pacific in the northern portion of our country where the Republican vote is strong, which seriously handicaps a Republican administration. A Republican president cannot safely count on the support of representatives in either House from several of the northwestern states.

No two classes of people could be more unlike than the Democrats of the South and the Democrats of the East. The Democratic voters of the solid South are the offspring of three or four generations of American-born people, largely Anglo-Saxon; colored labor kept the immigrants of the mixed bloods of Southern Europe out of the southland. The people of the South, city, town and country, on the highways and in the backwoods, for more than a half century, have voted the Democratic ticket, with something near a religious conviction. The vote for Mr. Hoover in the last presidential election did not indicate a change in political principles or convictions, but was the expression of righteous indignation. It was not voting the Republican ticket, so much, as it was voting against an insult to political decency. It was a loud and just protest against Tammany Hall and its liquor candidate.

The Southern States were dry by an overwhelming majority; not only legally, but conscientiously and religiously dry. The southland was dominated by some of the finest blood and breeding in all the broad land, and to have a group of foreigners, made up of Tammany Hall type, come into the national convention and put over on them a man so utterly foreign in culture, convictions, ideals and character to themselves, was more than they could endure. It is almost impossible to conceive of classes of people more unlike than the one hundred percent American Democrats of North and South Carolina, Virginia, Alabama, Georgia, Mississippi, Texas, Tennessee, Arkansas and Kentucky, and the immigrant Democrats of Chicago and New York City. The former are of the best citizenship of the land, with some strong prejudices, no

Is the World Growing Worse? 53

doubt; the latter are largely foreign-born, who are without any knowledge or care for the convictions, ideals and standards of the southern people. The East will vote for a Democratic Governor and a Republican President; note the last presidential election. A number of times New York City has elected Al Smith for governor of the State of New York, but in the presidential election they gave a Republican majority against him in the state, city, his own county and precinct.

Notwithstanding all of this, there were many otherwise excellent people in the South so deeply prejudiced, so thoroughly married to their party, that they shut their eyes and ears to the corruption of Tammany Hall, the wetness of the nominee, the constant effort of Romanism to dominate this country, and voted for Smith. I know of one religious weekly in a southern state that lost three thousand subscribers because of one editorial against the liquor traffic candidate. Contemplate that! This was a church paper supported by the most prominent families of the denomination the journal represented, yet they stopped the paper, forced the editor to resign, because he warned them against the possibilities of the curse of the saloon being thrust upon us. Most discouraging! It is difficult to realize that we have such professed Christians in Protestantism.

A few days ago I was in conversation with a friend of mine, a staunch, dyed-in-the wool Democrat. He insists that rum and Rome have had charge of the Democratic donkey, but that the faithful beast will kick himself loose and get back into control of the real Democracy in time to elect a Democratic president in 1932. This same friend also suggested that the wet and dry element in the Republican party will pull the elephant in two separate parts, and so spill their political beans that the Democrats will have a walk-over in the next presidential campaign.

This writer is not a prophet, nor will he undertake to forecast the future; the thing we deplore is, the possibility of the breaking up of the old political parties and the organization of a strong party of radicals. Unfortunately, our great cities have come to be a powerful, dominating force in politics; they swarm with a foreign element that is largely under the influence of a foreign combination of Pope-Emperor. They know and care nothing for high American ideals; they stand for unlicensed liberty, and want the saloon back with all of the degradation it breeds; and in these days when statesmen are few and politicians are many, eager for power, there is great danger that men who aspire to office, will sell their birthright for a mess of pottage that sickens the nation, and, eventually turns the wheels of progress backward, break down the republic, destroy our democratic principles and bring on a period of degradation, possibly revolution and bloodshed.

Nothing could be more unfortunate for the political life of this nation, than the fact that both political parties are powerfully influenced by the voting power of our great cities, largely under the control and direction of corrupt and conscienceless politicians who are dominated by puissant and corrupt interests.

There is a very powerful population in

this country known as the "underworld." This aggregation of humanity is easily handled by corrupt politicians. The inhabitants of the underworld are voters who can be rallied at any, and all times, by selfish interests and against men and measures for the uplift and betterment of social and moral conditions. There is an element of people in the country that are little better in anything of a spiritual nature, than the underworld. They are selfish and largely live off of human degradation. They do not object, but rather foster men and measures that contribute to their financial advantage, out of the degradation of the humbler and poorer elements of society.

There is a large element of what is known as the "better classes" who are so busy with their own affairs that they take little interest in politics. It is difficult to arouse them with any sort of enthusiasm to unite with patriotic and moral forces against demagogues and measures that are wholly evil in tendency and influence. This element of the better class are largely members of the church; they live very decent lives; they are of the spirit of the priest Jesus describes, who saw the wounded man who fell among thieves, was left stranded, and "passed by on the other side." This large class of very respectable people, who have a high appreciation of themselves, make but little contribution to the election of high class, patriotic men to office, moral tendency in legislation, the enforcement of law, and the general betterment of the civic life of the nation. They feel themselves almost too good to go down into the multitudes and help to fight out the practical battles of life for the improvement of social conditions and the uplift and betterment of the struggling masses.

One fortunate feature in the political life of the nation is the fact that we have come to have a very large element of excellent people who no longer wear the collar, and leap in obedience to the whip of any political party. They are men and women who are thinkers, who are quite alive to untoward conditions in the republic, who are disgusted with scheming politicians, who are constantly seeking power and pelf, rather than the general welfare of the people at large. This class of people are not slaves of any party. They are on the lookout for statesmen rather than listening to the soapbox orators of political factions. They want men of intelligence and high moral standards for leadership and the legislation of laws for the righteous government of nations, the proper distribution of wealth, and the securing of equal opportunity for all men of all classes to find employment and earn a competent living for themselves and their dependents. This more intelligent and thoughtful class are becoming tired and disgusted with the endless war that goes on between the old political parties, not so much for the improvement of conditions and the welfare of the people, but for office, each party fighting for power, and the pie counter, rather than for developments of the highest interests of the nation, and the contentment and happiness of the masses of the people.

The political outlook of the nation is not auspicious. Selfish millionaires, who have neither the fear of God nor the love of humanity, are contributing vast sums of money to rally under their black banners the most dangerous forces of the nation; to

Is the World Growing Worse? 59

place incompetent and selfish men in high positions of influence who will not, nor cannot, legislate and guide the affairs of the nation for the general betterment of the people, the lifting up and maintenance of high moral standards, and the quickening of spiritual influence and intuitions which make possible prosperity, peace and good will among men.

There must be an improvement in the leadership of the old parties; more clear-seeing, unselfish statesmanship and less of demagogery or there will be a revolt from the old parties of the better class of citizens which, perhaps, will not be sufficiently strong to elect representatives to their liking; meanwhile, those elements with a strong socialistic and communistic tendency are growing rapidly, and what the immediate, or the more distant future of the nation may be, would be difficult to prognosticate. When we speak of the immediate future we are thinking of the next four years; when we speak of the more distant future we are speaking of fifteen or twenty years hence. One thing appears absolutely certain: there must soon come very decided improvements for the better, or there will come rapid and fearful conditions far worse than the present. The tendencies now appear to be downward rather than upward. We have reached a place where there ought to be a nation-wide awakening for a great forward movement for honest, and patriotic men in office, and the relegation of self-seeking politicians who, like vultures, would feed and fatten upon the ruin of their fellowbeings.

CHAPTER VI.

THE MENACE OF THE MILLIONAIRE.

I think it will be very generally believed by those who know anything of economic and social conditions in this nation, that the vast accumulation of wealth in the hands of, and under the control of, a few people, and the painful poverty of the masses, offers one of the most serious problems our statesmen can contemplate.

The important question confronting those who guide the Ship of State, is not how shall we so control and direct the business and commerce of the country so as to increase the wealth of the millionaires but, what can be done to give employment to millions of idle men who are eager for work at wages sufficient to keep their families from pinching want—from actual starvation.

No land or government ever offered such opportunity to the whole people for the honest securing of the necessaries, and many of the comforts of life, as this country. For more than a century toil found its rich rewards in this broad land. Hundreds of thousands of the honest yeomanry of this country, with axe and hoe and plow, worked their way up from poverty to modest wealth. They have furnished as fine a citizenry as the world ever saw. They were self-respecting, in the best sense, neither aristocratic or plebeian; they were democratic in the truest sense. This nation has experienced equality and fraternity in a high degree. The highest classes, the only nobility, have been those men and women who have most unselfishly and wisely served their fellowbeings.

For many decades in the early history of this new world, men did not strive for great wealth. They worked hard, economized and planned for comfortable homes, the education of their children, and a competency for their declining years. The increase of population was so rapid, the demands for homes, furniture and the tools of toil were so great, that many men in the various manufactories and trades became honestly rich.

One of the first great efforts to corner and control one of the rich resources of nature was that made by the Standard Oil Company. The men who organized this enterprise were just as determined to own this great industry as Japan is to have a large slice of the rich lands of Manchuria. Its plans well laid, it marched into action and crushed into ruin and bankruptcy all oppositions to its insatiate greed. A number of prosperous men who found themselves in hopeless ruin committed suicide.

There was a great cry against this conscienceless octopus, but it proved as shrewd as it was merciless, and bought the favor of politicians, schools and churches. Standard Oil has built one of the most skeptical universities in the world; it has helped to erect a four million dollar church building for the preaching of modern liberalism, that strikes a death blow at every fundamental doctrine of the Holy Scriptures. We doubt if there are any more sinners won to Christ at this vast altar to popular unbelief than there are in Bolshevik halls in Petrograd dedicated to atheism, and revolt against the Bible, and the God of the Bible. Every sort of trusts and cornering of the necessaries of life have followed in the wake of Standard Oil. We have the coal trust, the lumber trust, the meat trust, the fruit trust, the steel trust, the clothing trust, the shoe trust, tobacco trust, farming implement trust, and combinations for the control, shipping and marketing of almost everything that goes into the supply of the needs of civilization. *Crush competition* is the slogan of big business.

The money power of this nation fixes the tariffs, regulates the prices paid for the raw materials, controls the manufacturing, distribution and prices paid by the consumers of the necessaries of life, all so directed that the poor become poorer, and the rich become richer. Now we have the chain stores dragging the money net from ocean to ocean in this country, gathering the dimes and dollars of the people to pour them by countless millions into the coffers of a few men. For example: Here is a city of eighteen thousand people; it is a prosperous little center of trade and traffic. It cannot escape the hungry eyes of the vultures of predatory wealth. One of five different combinations of chain stores is set up in this city. The managers of these stores buy

Is the World Growing Worse? 65

in such vast quantities, and often goods of an inferior quality, that they can undersell the local merchants; and the people pour into them. The home merchants who pay the taxes, build the schools, support the churches and make the little city a prosperous and comfortable place to live, are driven out of business; the churches and all of the institutions of the town suffer. The money received by the chain stores week by week, is shipped away to some great city, and never comes back; so far as the people who earned and spent it are concerned, it is out of circulation forever; had just as well been dumped into the river. The result is, that home banks are closed, merchants bankrupt, a few suicides, energetic young men are forced to leave home and find employment elsewhere, the planing mill is idle, lumber rots in the stack, there is no building going on, no sale of furniture to furnish new homes, while the new census reveals the fact that the population of the town is less than it was ten years ago, stores are empty, the people who own cottages and bungalows cannot rent them, taxes are heavy; they try to sell their vacant houses, there are no buyers; men mope about wondering what has brought such stagnation to their town.

The answer is simple and easy; they have sent all of their money out of their town and community through the chain stores into the insatiate pockets of the millionaires of New York City. And so this drainage goes on from year to year, impoverishing the people, giving greater wealth and power to greed. It comes to pass that money, not principles, dictates and controls commerce, politics, the school and the church. Millionaires can buy up a great political party, put it in their vest pocket like a watch, or a trinket, pull it out, wind it up and dictate and control men as if they were slaves. Millionaires control the public press of the country, own the papers and magazines, and direct the flow of corrupting literature which inundates the land with mental rubbish and moral poison.

We now have a combination of multi-millionaires united together to break down the prohibition law of the land and bring back the liquor traffic upon us; and they are bold enough to tell us that the taxation

Is the World Growing Worse? 67

of liquor would relieve them of their heavy income taxes. They are not only willing to degrade the poor laboring men with drunkenness, but want them to pay the expenses of financing the government while they are relieved of the burden, and left to luxuriate in their wealth. We have in this nation some most excellent people of large means who are servants of God and humanity. Their philanthropies are generous and wisely distributed, and they well deserve the honor and respect bestowed upon them; nevertheless, it is quite true that a very large percent of the donations of the very rich never touch the sore spot in society, and increase, rather than solve, our economic and social problems. It requires no argument to prove that it were far better for all the people that there should be many millions of small prosperous farmers, mechanics and merchants than that they should be bankrupted, their farms and stores taken over by the banks that have furnished them money they can never repay, the land bought up by rich trusts, cultivated with machinery and the people left in idleness and gaunt hunger.

The American people will never make good peaceable serfs. These United States have been, and are, the land of opportunity; no other country in the history of the world, since Abraham marched into Canaan, has been such a land of promise as this vast expanse of territory stretching from the Atlantic to the Pacific, and from the northern Lakes to the Gulf of Mexico, filled with everything that man needs to supply both comforts and luxuries. But human greed is money mad, and is bringing on a crisis which promises anything but prosperity and peace.

It is almost impossible to punish the very rich for any crime they see fit to commit. They can break banks, water stocks, rob the public, marry and divorce at will, rape and debauch young women, walk roughshod over society, violate law, then employ shrewd, lawless lawyers, postpone trial, change venue, hire witnesses, bribe juries, take their cases from court to court, wear out prosecution and laugh at justice.

Any thoughtful student of conditions in the economic situation of this country, and the present drift, will tell you that there is every indication that, as the years go by, and very rapidly, the money of this country will be owned and controlled by a very few, and the masses of the populace will be dangerously poor. Poor, hard-worked people can become cowed and dull, but when awakened, they are extremely emotional and their emotions kindle into anger; they become unreasonable and desperate—then woe be to those they believe have wronged and impoverished them!

CHAPTER VII.

DOES THE PRESENT OUTLOOK PROMISE WORLD PEACE?

That the world is war weary is evident. It has been taught by sad experience that one of the serious features of war is the aftermath—the heavy taxes, the human wreckage, with widows and orphans who must be looked after and cared for by the governments who have engaged in war. Intelligent, patriotic, Christian men of all nations are ready to rise in protest against war and the ravages it brings in the destruction of property, the waste of life, and the burdens beneath which the living must stagger after wars are over.

Wars do not bring peace; finally, one of the nations engaged in war is conquered. Their physical and financial powers are exhausted, but hatred and animosity are intensified, and the conquered people, for the present, smother and conceal as best they can, their thirst for revenge, and the impatence with which they wait to repay their conquerors with all accrued interest possi-

Is the World Growing Worse? 71

ble. Three or four generations of conquered people can be born, live and die and pass on from generation to generation, the hatred of their victorious foes, each succeeding generation hoping that the time of bloody retaliation may come. It seems impossible for a people to forget the ravages of an invading foe, the wreck and ruin they bring with sword and torch; they nurse and pass their hatred and desire for revenge on through the centuries.

Unfortunately, these bitter memories and longings for a settlement of accounts exist among many of the different nations of Europe, as well as in the Orient. In the heart of India there is a grim and abiding longing which cannot die, to break the British yoke. Mahatmi Ghandi is a marvelous diplomat. He knew very well that India, untrained for war, and without arms and ammunition, could not cope with the powers of Great Britain. It is not improbable that he might have resorted to other means than his little spinning-wheel, if he had at his command three or four millions of well trained, well equipped soldiers, with a thousand modern airships, and a fleet of war vessels that could have met the British navy with strong probabilities of victory. Without any of these forces, he was compelled to think in other terms than those of war. "As a man thinketh in his heart, so is he." No doubt this remarkable little man in his breechclout, is a man for peace; peaceable methods are the only methods by which he can hope to secure the ends desired.

Anything approaching brotherly love between France and Germany is quite impossible, without the peoples of these nations being "born again," recreated. Unfortunately, we see no indications of such sweep of supernatural manifestation and power among the people of either nation mentioned. There is deep-seated hatred, and should favorable opportunity offer, either nation will undoubtedly seek to settle old scores. We doubt if there has been a time within the past century when, in spite of the diplomatic courtesy on the surface, there was more of hatred and fear among the nations of earth, than at the present time.

In the October number of *The Forum*, there is a very interesting article by Mr. George N. Shuster, who writes under the

Is the World Growing Worse? 73

caption of "Communism, or the Catholic Church." While we do not sympathize with much he has to say, we are forcefully impressed with the long introductory paragraph which we share with our readers:

"Fifteen years ago the nations of the West were fighting for victory; today they are fighting for life. That is, I think, the most accurate possible summary of recent history. Now for some of the details. Russia, after a million murders, in the hands of Stalin, perfectly willing to do a million more if necessary. Germany starving, with hundreds of thousands of families eating at soup kitchens and ridding themselves wholesale of unborn offspring. Britain gradually succumbing to industrial anemia. Italy afraid to whimper, but the girls who sew laces for the American market get fifteen cents a day and furnish their own thread. South Central Europe a fantastic collection of boundaries and of businesses none of which could pay a nickel on the dollar. The colonial countries, out of which cowboys took millions in hard cash a generation ago, worse than stone broke. And even the United States, dividend clipper to mankind, so short of work that the American Federation of Labor is afraid to publish what it knows and so short of markets that the cash register is an extravagance."

This is a rather gloomy pen picture, but hardly any one acquainted with the facts would dare intimate that it is overdrawn. While statesmen and churchmen must hope for the best, they are compelled to face facts.

On July 5, 1931, there appeared in *The Lexington Leader*, published in Lexington, Ky., the following with reference to utterances by Senator Borah. It deserves thoughtful consideration:

"Senator Borah, who, as chairman of the foreign relations committee of the senate, holds, next to the President, the most powerful position in the government, in a recent article discusses the proposal to cancel the war debts in order to buy European disarmament—

Is the World Growing Worse? 75

a really childish suggestion. He points out that European armaments, which have grown enormously since the World War closed and which are costing between four and five billions of dollars annually, rest squarely upon certain conditions and a state of mind which cannot be changed by making Europe a present of 10 billions of dollars, levying upon the American taxpayer to cover such obligations.

"The war left in Europe a legacy of hate, of jealousy, of fear, and of suspicion and the so-called treaties of peace, written while the nations were suffering from fresh wounds and filled with fierce enmity, created new causes of hostility. They drew arbitrary boundaries, moved populations about from one sovereignty to another, broke up once powerful kingdoms, alienated large territories, and sought to fix a state of servitude upon defeated peoples."

"Senator Borah quotes a recent statement from the trenchant pen of the distinguished editor of the Journal de Geneve, Mr. William Martin. He says:

'The war, which directly created the difficulties with which we are struggling, indirectly prevents their solution because of its psychological results. The nations are divided by political questions; these differences of opinion make them fear the return of war and consequently turn them away from military disarmament, without which there can be no pacification of public opinion and no tariff disarmament, without which we cannot hope for prosperity nor, consequently, for social, political and moral calm. All these things hold together.'

"France has been most insistent upon cancellation. What is her particular attitude toward disarmament? Her memorandum, just dispatched to the secretariat of the league, declares that until there is an international army ready to enforce the Versailles treaty she cannot undertake to cut her present establishment in any respect.

"The French president said the other day:

'France has a right to think that so long as the League of Nations, to whose existence she is so faithfully attached, has not at its disposal a military force sufficient to impose the execution of its decisions on those not disposed to bow voluntarily before them, she must watch out, be on her guard, and count on herself.'

"Senator Borah points out that the present situation is due to the fact that Europe is living under the shadow of a treaty based upon the principle of restraint and of repression, limiting, and, indeed, crushing the aspirations of peoples, and calling for bayonets as the only means of its execution. This doctrine of force, inherent in the Versailles treaty, precludes for the time any hope of a real reduction in armaments. If conditions are unchanged every dollar of indebtedness remitted by this country would mean another dollar to be put into the military and naval establishments of Europe.

"Senator Borah concludes:

'If there is no remedy for this situation, then the arguments for cancellation based on the economic recovery of Europe, upon mercy for the overtaxed and underfed, upon increasing the purchasing power of millions of people and creating thereby markets for our manufacturers and our farmers all fall to the ground.'

"The logic is invincible whatever may be thought about the desirability, or feasibility, of total cancellation as the purchase price of European disarmament."

Desirable as peace is, and horrible as war is, conditions exist in Europe that, throughout the past, have fostered strife and finally, have produced a state of mind that leads to bloody conflict. Reason would of course, insist on peace at almost any

Is the World Growing Worse? 79

price, but selfish, angry men cease to reason and resort to force.

Just at this time, the outlook for peace—protracted, settled peace—is not auspicious. The state of mind in this country is not as courageous and bouyant as it was when the World War was at the height of its bloody effusion. Then men believed that, finally, the war would end and the dove of universal peace would spread its wings over a warless world, which had been taught by the shock of battle, a waste of life and the destruction of property produced by the toil of the centuries, to war no more, to become lovers of their fellowbeings; that a sort of universal altruism would unite the nations of the earth into a sympathetic and kindly brotherhood. They have been sadly mistaken; there are more men under arms in Europe today than there were when the war broke out in 1914, and the inventors and chemists of all nations are busy seeking after the materials of war which will annihilate armies and devastate nations.

The sad fact is, the world very largely is at war against God. It is in a state of rebellion against the King of the universe.

It is practically impossible for men to be at peace with each other, when they refuse to be at peace with God.

In his last public address to his people, we find an exhortation from King David, well worth our consideration. He had assembled the captains of his army, and the elders of Israel into a great multitude; he is going to resign his throne and bid his people a final farewell. He reached the climax of his address with these profound words: "Now therefore in the sight of all Israel the congregation of the Lord, and in the audience of our God, keep and seek all the commandments of the Lord your God; that ye may posses this good land, and leave it for an inheritance for your children after you forever."

We understand that their title deed to the goodly country which God had given them was careful obedience to His commandments. Israel soon forgot the exhortation of their king. They broke their covenant with God; they trampled upon His commandments. They refused His mercy and directly, their hills were covered with the tents of their pagan foes, and their val-

Is the World Growing Worse? 81

leys trembled beneath the charge of the chariots of their victorious enemies. Their captive people hung their silent harps upon the weeping willows of Babylon, and they went away in chains to die the helpless slaves of their captive masters.

If the nations would be at peace with themselves, they should first of all, and most of all, seek peace with God. We look in vain for any appearance or indication of any sort for a spiritual awakening, and a revival of the religion of Jesus Christ in any part of Europe.

Within recent months one of the great powers, Japan, has ruthlessly violated the covenant into which she entered with other nations to preserve world peace. She has refused to listen to the pleadings, entreaties and counsel of the representatives of those nations with which she signed the peace compact. She has invaded a neighbor nation under the scourge of the fearful inundation with millions of her people on the verge of starvation, suffering also from internal strife, and quite unprepared to protect herself from a powerful and well trained foe, and actuated by ruthless greed has bombarded a great city, destroying hundreds of millions of property, and thousands of unprotected, helpless women and children, has seized, in addition to this, a vast territory of land rich in resources and while carrying forward this aggressive and bloody invasion, has smiled in the face of protest, all the while arguing that she has no selfish motives.

The Disarmament Conference made eloquent speeches and many suggestions tending toward world peace at its meeting some months ago, but during the following discussions it became evident to observers that there is not the slightest probability that any of the great world powers will disarm, or cease to prepare for a coming conflict that may possibly surpass, with blood and fire, anything known in the history of the world. A world at war with God is certain to continue at war with itself.

CHAPTER VIII.

OUR YOUNG PEOPLE ARE NOT BEING TAUGHT RELIGION IN THE SCHOOLS.

Several millions of our young people come to voting age each year. Those who are now in the colleges and universities of the nation will soon be in control of the affairs of the nation. Young people now in school will be largely what their teachers make them. They will believe what they are taught. They will think the thoughts of their instructors. "As a man thinketh in his heart, so is he."

Thought kindles desire; desire leads to action; repeated actions form habits; habits build character, and character determines the weal or woe of the nation, and finally, fixes destiny. Are the moral and spiritual standards set up and inculcated in the great schools of this country such as will produce the best type of citizens?

I quote a significant passage from "Studies in the Prophecy of Jeremiah," by G. Campbell Morgan.

"There may be apparent material prosperity without moral cleansing, but it never abides. It is the old story, uttered over and over again, perhaps most terribly put a generation ago by the iron Duke Wellington, when the education of a people was being discussed, and he said: 'If you educate these children apart from religion, you will make them clever devils.' It was the rough, uncouth language, if you like, of a man of war, but it was the language of a prophet, of a man who had perfect understanding of human nature. If you have not dealt with the inspirational centers, as well as with the external things of life, the garden will become a slum again."

Not long since, a scientific communist boasted that he could make and plant an explosive, with a time clock attachment, in the loop at Chicago, and be five hundred miles away before it blew up countless millions of dollars worth of property and killed some tens of thousands of people. His statement was doubtless true. The discoveries of modern science, with its powerful destructive forces in the hands of men, who have been taught to hate the word, "God," and to look upon themselves and their fellowbeings as soulless, irresponsible animals, have brought us to a period in the progress of our boasted civilization, when we may fully appreciate the emphatic words of the iron Duke.

I give you here an editorial published some time ago in The Baltimore Southern Methodist. It is from the very clear mind of the Editor of that excellent paper, Rev. Nolan B. Harmon.

THE FOURTH "R."

"Down at Charlottesville they have an Institute of Public Affairs every summer at the University of Virginia. They talk about some things in the heavens above, and considerably more in the earth beneath, but always get into the papers on account of the row they start over prohibition. But this year a note was sounded by Dean Luther A. Weigle of the Yale Divinity School concerning about as public an affair as can possibly be, and that is, the attitude of the public schools toward religion. The Dean practically says that there is no attitude; the public schools ignore the whole question. 'This,' he adds, 'inevitably conveys to children a negative suggestion. They cannot help but notice the omission. It is bound to discredit religion in their minds. It is natural for them to conclude that religion is negligible, or unimportant, or irrelevant to the real business of life.'

"Of course this attitude is negative. If a Jewish boy objects to the reading of the New Testament or the Lord's Prayer; if a Roman Catholic is against the Bible in school chapel; if the son of an atheist complains of morning prayer in the school room, what happens? Nothing. These are stopped. The school board or trustees are afraid that some one will say they are "mixing Church and State;' that religious liberty will be taken from a minority—which should be protected in a state supported school. The majority can get along without the objectionable feature, and, in short, the negative course is the one of least resistance.

"Now we will go as far as anyone to protect minority rights, and these must always be respected both in Church and State, but is not this negative attitude of the public school a *positive* injustice to all for the sake of a few? Is not opposition to religious instruction in school a sort of sectarian faith itself? Why should it be respected more than the will of the many who call for the time-honored principles of American morality to be inculcated in children? Our very public schools themselves are the result of the ages of God-fearing ancestors who were taught religion in school. One wonders what the ages to come will show when the boys and girls now getting no view at all of religion and morality shall take the nation over. Religious training may be *negative* but passions are exceedingly positive and the public schools had better awaken to it.

"Whatever the State does, let the

Church keep its own schools and colleges and make them places where learning is shot through with Christianity. Add to the three 'R's' one more: RELIGION. Without it there is no heart in the whole process—and no hope."

The facts indicated here are so patent that comment is unnecessary. The schools of the country, from the primary department to graduation from the greatest universities, are neglecting the religious training of the child and young people who are soon to be the controlling forces of the nation. We clip the following from Zion's Herald:

"There is not any too much intelligent attention being expended on the training of the little child's spiritual side. A 500-page volume on 'The Nature and Needs of the Child' had no word in its index like 'God,' 'Christ,' 'Prayer,' and only two slight references to religion. Glands and games, intelligence quotas, and a good many other elements of child development have received exhaustive and scholarly

Is the World Growing Worse?

attention, but on the actual religious nurture, none too much brains or money has been spent. While the average expenditure of 30,000,000 members of Protestant churches for their church schools is $0.05 each a year, and while the average city church spends $1.46 per capita for music, and $0.48 per capita for all the children's and young people's work, it cannot be reasonably said that too much is being done for the rising generation, and at least with any success, and as far as its *religious* education is concerned."

We must not forget that there is much being taught in the schools that is decidedly irreligious. This is not only true on the part of professors who worship at the shrine of Evolution, who look upon themselves and their students as well developed, irresponsible animals, but there is, perhaps, no more dangerous teaching going on today than in the class-room of the professors of Psychology. Not long since, a Professor of Psychology in one of the great universities, said to his class one morning, "If you young people have anything that you call religion, you had just as well throw it overboard now, for you will not have it when you shall have finished this course of study." In the same university another professor said, "If you young people have anything that you call souls, you may hitch them outside before coming to this lecture room. You will have no use for them in here."

There is much of this kind of sneer, not only at religion, but at the idea of the existence of a human soul. The Christian people of this nation are heavily taxed to support institutions where, in teaching and spirit, the Christian religion is a subject of ridicule.

CHAPTER IX.

WHAT OUR YOUNG PEOPLE ARE BEING TAUGHT IN THE SCHOOLS.

Rev. William P. King, D.D., Editor of Books of the Southern Methodist Publishing House, Nashville, Tenn., has brought out a book with the suggestive title, "Behaviorism—A Battle Line!" He has brought into his service a number of the very eminent scholars, teachers and preachers of the country. Dr. King renders a very important service to the reading public in preparing and sending forth this timely discussion of some of the most important subjects that can claim the attention of devout and, I may say, of decent people.

The book contains a discussion of, and protest against, the materialistic philosophy of Behaviorism. The high priest of this cult is one Dr. J. B. Watson who claims to be a master in the realm of psychology. Some of his books have attracted wide attention and received unusual praise. One of the New York dailies acclaims one of his principal productions as "Perhaps the most important book ever written." Another daily says, "It marks an epoch in the intellectual history of man."

This new book edited by Dr. King, published and sent forth by the Cokesbury Press, of Nashville, Tenn., should have a wide and thoughtful reading. We give here a quotation from the discussion of the subject involved by Dr. King. It reads as follows:

> "The most active and perilous foe of religion today is what is termed the new psychology of behaviorism. Its definite purpose is announced by a modern advocate: 'Religion hitherto has been wounded by science on the surface of the skin only. It has been reserved for psychology to enter the arena and to deliver the deathblow. When the combat is ended we shall hear no more of God or the soul or religion; all the apparatus of religion will be scrapped, and mankind, free from the incubus of false beliefs, will march to the conquest of the universe.'
>
> "According to Behaviorism all ex-

Is the World Growing Worse?

hortations to choose between good and evil, to live in accord with the highest ideals, to cheerfully acquiesce in sacrifice for the common good, to meditate upon the true values of life, to make an eager quest for the true and beautiful and good, are addressed to a phantom.

"Faith, hope, love, truth, beauty, and goodness all vanish into thin mist.

"The human personality has no-value, because there is no personality.

"Why should there be any more concern over the loss of life in a train wreck than over the destruction of the engine?

"Darrow and Mencken and other Behaviorists hold that in reality the criminal is not responsible and could not have done otherwise, and at the same time plead with society or with a jury to change their attitude toward the criminal. But if the criminal cannot do otherwise than he does, neither can society or the jury."

The reader can readily see from this definition that Behaviorism, as it is being taught in schools and widely read by the public, is a most dangerous menace to everything that is safe and sane, pure and good in our American life. The introduction to the book is written by Josiah Morse, Ph.D., of the University of South Carolina, located at Columbia. We give an excerpt from the introduction. It certainly should provoke serious thought and earnest protest.

"Finally, I wish to repeat the warning I uttered before the Southern Society for Philosophy and Psychology. When the Sophists taught the post-war youths of Athens that the individual is a law and a measure unto himself, that there is no authority or universal norm, the far-seeing Socrates realized that the inevitable outcome of such a doctrine would be social disintegration and confusion resulting in the downfall of Athenian civilization. Our present-day Sophists, with equal recklessness are preaching equally disturbing doctrines to the present generation. And like their ancient prototypes they are

Is the World Growing Worse?

gathering around them youths, and in this day maidens too, who delight to hear that the old gods are dead and the old beliefs with their checks and balances and controls are without validity and foundation in fact; that man is merely a two-legged goat who has been absurdly and unnaturally conditioned by the psycho-social environment projected from the far-distant and ignorant past; that the time has come for them to recondition themselves and strike off the antiquated shackles—to give full rein to their impulses, instincts, and tendencies, or, as the college flappers say, to liberate their libido and 'can' their complexes."

One of the strong chapters of the book is written by Prof. William McDougall, of Duke University, located at Durham, N. C. He writes under the head of "The Psychology they teach in New York." The reader will find it quite startling, especially those readers who have not kept abreast of much destructive thinking and writing that has been pouring in a stream of poison from the public press for the past few decades. Dr. McDougall says:

> "In the sphere of domestic life its deductions are boldly applied. And here it does not hesitate to take over from the utterly incompatible teachings of the Freudian school whatever is most disturbing and destructive to traditional belief and practice. Tradition holds that the monogamic family is the foundation of the State and the institution most necessary and conducive to human welfare, happiness, and progress. Behaviorism attacks it at every point. The relations between man and woman it would reduce to nothing more than one means for securing sensual gratifications; and those relations between the sexes are best which will produce the maximum amount of such gratification. Romantic love, marital fidelity, and pre-marital chastity for either sex, all these become absurd and pernicious survivals. Watson has foretold that within fifty years marriage will have ceased to be

an American institution; and there can be little doubt that if his theory of human nature could be shown to be true, or if, in spite of its falsity, it should continue to spread as it has spread in the last decade, his forecast will be realized."

Dr. McDougall says further: These teachings are being broadcasted among teachers and college students, and very correctly suggests the destructive effect of such teaching. Let me quote just what he does say:

"Do I, then, suggest that the terrible crime rate of America is the effect of the famous sarbon theory? I do not go quite so far as that. But I do suggest and contend that the crude materialistic theory of human nature, the theory that man is a machine and nothing more, taught dogmatically every year to hundreds of thousands of innocent school-teachers and college students, cannot fail in the long run to contribute very considerably to the decay of morals and the increase of crime. For it is a theory utterly incompatible with any view of man as a responsible moral being and utterly incompatible with any religion that the plain man could recognize as such; a theory which represents man as incapable of choosing between good and evil, as the purely passive sport of circumstances over which he has no control; a theory which, if it is accepted, must make all talk of self-control, of self-improvement, of purposes and ideals seem sheer nonsense, survivals from an age of naive ignorance."

We would impress upon our readers the fact that however the church may be neglecting to inculcate high moral ideals and spiritual truth into the mind and thought of the rising generation of young people, the unbelieving world is quite busy with every sort of propaganda that is not only destructive of all evangelical faith, but is bound to produce fearful effects upon the people who will directly control the destiny of the nation. It means ultimately the destruction of the home and the church, and a revel and riot of wickedness of every kind.

We add two more short excerpts from Dr. McDougall's very interesting and illuminating discussion of the Psychology they teach in New York.

"I have assigned a certain responsibility in this matter to the city of New York. This assignment is justified primarily because the teaching I criticise has emanated chiefly from the halls of learning of that city and especially from Columbia University, where the former head of the department of psychology, Dr. McKeen Cattell (who may claim to be the spiritual begetter of Thorndike and Watson), set that department upon the narrow and 'strictly scientific' lines which have led to such deplorable results. But the responsibility lies more widely. New York is the financial and intellectual metropolis of the nation, and whatever comes out of New York enjoys an immense prestige.

"Even the South, America's pathetic home of lost causes, her last refuge for piety and conservatism, is rapidly becoming mechanized, with cement roads and noisy silent-policemen in every town, plumbing in every room, and the sarbon theory in every school. A Southern teacher recently complained to me that, wherever he goes, he finds Behaviorism rampant in the schools, and that, because he cannot accept it, he finds himself regarded by his colleagues as hopelessly out-of-date."

We most heartily recommend the book from which we have quoted to preachers, college professors, school-teachers and the public, generally. The people ought to know just what sort of moral seed is being sown in the intellectual and moral life of the young people of this nation. As we read the thoughtful discussions contained in the book we are reminded of the closing sentence of one of the chapters in the French Revolution written by Thomas Carlyle. He is describing the gathering clouds that broke into a storm of fire and blood over France, and writes "They had sown to the wind, and as sure as God is true, and His Word is true, they had to reap the whirlwind."

The book from which we have been quoting contains 376 pages, clear print, on excellent paper, well bound, and can be had of The Southern Methodist Publishing House, Nashville, Tenn.

Suppose a group of Christian students attending a university come under the influence of these Behavioristic teachers, should become distressed over their religious faith and on Sabbath they go to church for help and reassurance that the scriptural foundations upon which they have built are absolutely sure, but the preacher stands in the sacred desk and assures them that the Old Testament is simply folklore, that Jesus was not virgin born, that there is no redemptive merit in his death, that he was not resurrected, and much else that is being taught in many pulpits today. Would such students receive any help from such preacher for the support and strengthening of their Christian faith? There is much teaching of this character in many pulpits in our land today.

Do the facts recorded in these chapters with reference to what our young people are being taught encourage us to believe that we may confidently expect the world to grow better?

CHAPTER X.

THE HARVEST.

We have been taught in sacred Writ that, "Whatsoever a man soweth, that shall he also reap." History and experience prove this scriptural statement to be absolutely true. The same may be applied to the teachings in our colleges and universities. We give our readers something of the harvest that is growing, and furnishing seed for a fearful reproduction and a larger reaping. The reader will remember that, in the preceding chapter, we quote extensively from a distinguished scholar who tells us something of what is being taught in the schools of New York City. Just before Christmas of the past year, we clipped from one of the leading dailies the following description of conditions in New York City, in preparation for the celebration of the Yuletide Season:

New York, Nov. 26.—"The shop windows here are filling up with dollar teasers in anticipation of the holidays and from all indications this is going to be a bawdy Yule Season. Once-suppressed or forbidden literature is boldly displayed, toy shops filled with gambling devices, gangster equipment and leering dolls.

"The holiday literary bargains easily win first place. The book stores are putting ordinary fiction and standard editions in the background and moving their risque offerings right up against the plate glass. Tomes that once were sold secretly and at fancy prices may be bought from $1 up, and lie opened at their most revealing chapters in almost every window.

FOR PASSER-BY

"One shop in the Times Square district makes a practice of underlining in heavy ink the most flagrant examples of eroticism. Its windows are usually smeared with fingerprints, mute evidence of its attractions. A downtown department store has been going in for amatory classics in a big way and already has exhausted two huge shipments from an astonished publishing firm.

"The forbidden phonograph record business is at its peak and discs bearing vulgar songs, anatomical jokes and lewd after-dinner speeches are sold almost openly in scores of small shops. There is a growing supply of shameless motion-picture films for home use and the holiday demand is greater than ever before, according to the bootleg film dealers.

NUDES RAMPANT

"A canvass of the art shops reveals windows filled with nudes and lewdness rampant. Several Fifth-avenue houses feature paintings that leave nothing to the imagination and their impudicity cannot be laid to art as they are not 'old masters.' A shop in the theatrical district is attracting holiday gift seekers from all over town with its amazing collection of Rabelaisian prints. There is another that deals virtually exclusively in nudes and prints of erotomania. There are prices to fit every pocketbook.

"The Christmas card business is just opening up but appearances indicate that bawdy prints will rule. The majority of offerings in this rapidly growing business that have appeared on the market have to do with debauchery rather than snow and reindeer scenes. Santa Claus has developed a red nose and the frosty weather has nothing to do with its tint.

CORRUPTING YOUNG

"It is in the toy shops, however, that the pagan influence makes itself most strongly felt. Here, if in any place, one would expect to find old friends and old traditions preserved. Instead, mixed in among the standard toys, are dice games, wheels of chance, roulette layouts and every conceivable gambling device. The 1931 tots are going to be chance-takers if Santa Claus has anything to say about it.

"The background of the current trend toward shamelessness may be found on Broadway. That street and its attractions resemble an untended barnyard. A new era of vulgarity is beginning. Burlesque shows and their strip choruses are crowding in between the film houses and Tin Pan Alley song shops in almost every block. Forty-second street has reverted almost entirely into a super-bawdy Coney Island. Even the once costly flesh revues are playing at cut prices.

"The signs in front of these luridly plastered theaters are phrased in vulgar puns and the posters picture lewd ladies with all the abandon of their sisters on the front pages of the 25-cent 'Paris weeklies.' "

The above does not reflect credit on the powerful influence that Tammany Hall has in the political and moral life of our greatest American City. Out from this center of graft and moral corruption, comes an army of well-groomed, well-fed, pompous men to the various conventions of the political parties, every four years, to dictate to the decent people of this nation who shall be candidate for president of this great republic.

The reader must not for a moment, conclude that New York, alone, is so fearfully apostate and corrupt. It is possibly the worst, having a vast population made up of a very bad element of many nations who must be cared for because they furnish tremendous voting power for ambitious and corrupt politicians. Chicago follows closely in the lead of New York, and what I saw on the streets, and in pictures at the entrance of moving picture houses in Los Angeles this winter, would suggest that when it comes to the nude, the vulgar, and the output of unrestrained depravity, could scarcely be surpassed anywhere.

Some of the great city dailies are calling attention to, and crying out against the immorality that is deluging the centers of population. We give below excerpts from the New York Tribune, and Chicago Tribune, which are very suggestive:

"Two of America's leading newspapers point out dangers which unless changed may spell the doom of the nation. The New York Tribune has an article on 'The Immoralities of the Theater.' The writer says, 'The process of teaching moral lessons by de-

Is the World Growing Worse? 109

picting the filthy minutiæ of vice has done more harm than any single force that ever was let loose in the realms of literature and art. Plays that introduce the young to the society of the disreputable serve only to familiarize the minds of that audience with disreputable persons and nasty themes. Such plays carry the idea that love is above the law. Plays which diffuse such a subtle contamination as deleterious as impure air, as insidious as small-pox, should be forever banned.'

"The second article is from the Chicago Tribune and deals with the cigarette. It states that over one hundred billion cigarettes were smoked in America last year. This represents an increase of more than five billlion cigarettes smoked over the previous year, and the consumption of the same has more than doubled in the last ten years. This is possibly due to the fact that so many of the girls and women of the land have taken up the abominable habit.

"Yes, America is doomed unless

the movies, the theater, and smoking, and the disrespect for law are changed. Nations do not fall until their moral heart is shot through and through with immorality."—*Selected.*

When the floodgates of sin are open, and the people become degraded and thoroughly saturated with lewdness and vice of every kind, lawlessness becomes rampant, the foundations of society give way, and life and property are no longer sacred or safe. Note the following from one of the dailies:

New York, Nov. 20.—"The entire New York financial district—and the office of J. P. Morgan & Co. particularly—was today under one of the heaviest police guards ever assigned to to such duty as the result of a series of threatening letters.

"The letters, signed 'Communist,' were received not only by officials of Morgan & Co., but also by Harvey D. Gibson, chairman of the Emergency Unemployment Relief Committee; by officials of the New York Stock Exchange and of the Bankers' Trust Co.

GUARDS TREBLED

"The letters were turned over to the Department of Justice at Washington which immediately requested the heavy police guard.

"A number of detectives armed with tear gas bombs and riot guns were stationed in private automobiles along Broad street.

"Members of New York City's crack bomb squad were included in a detail of twenty detectives patroling the White building of the Morgan firm at Wall and Broad streets.

DYNAMITE SEIZED

"The uniformed force in the entire vicinity was trebled and a special watch was being kept over the Stock Exchange, the Sub-treasury building, Gibson's office at 55 Broad street, and other points in the financial district.

"At police headquarters, it was said extra precautions were being taken not only because of the letters but because one of five men, arrested four days ago with a large quantity of dynamite, was quoted as saying that it was to have been used as the 'opening gun' of a campaign against capitalism."

We see in the above something of the outcome of false teaching in the schools and universities of this country. It will be understood that we, by no means, lay these charges at the door of all the schools, but it is well known that comparatively few of the schools, as has been shown in the preceding chapters, lay any emphasis on religious teaching, or anything approaching a vital evangelical faith. Destroy the religious faith of the rising generation, take out of their thought a reverential fear of the God revealed in the Bible, and the result is bound to be sin of every kind, the loss of modesty, of reverence, of virtue, of respect for human, as well as divine law, and directly, there will arise a tide of lawlessness that not only means revolution, but the destruction and sweeping away of everything worth while in a Christian civilization.

CHAPTER XI.

TRYING TO GET RID OF GOD

An inspired writer, many centuries before the birth of Christ, wrote this emphatic statement: "The fool hath said in his heart, There is no God." Through all human history there has been a class of men who have tried to get rid of God; to put him entirely out of their thought, in fact, to annihilate him altogether. Their lives have been of a character that they have known, if there is a just and holy God, before whom they must render an account of their conduct, they could not escape his condemnation.

Atheists have labored long and assiduously to account for the universe and its splendid order, without an intelligent Creator. They have found this a difficult task. It is hard to convince thinking people that a universe so vast, containing the globe on which we live, with its marvelous adjustment and adaptation to our natural needs, could exist without an all-wise, omnipotent and compassionate Creator.

When Darwin came forward with his

theory of Evolution that, by gradual processes the universe, and the life in it, both animate and inanimate, animal and human, had gradually evolved itself into existence without the act and control of a divine Being, atheists, infidels, skeptics and agnostics greeted it with hilarity. No teaching has ever spread so rapidly among men as the hypothesis of Evolution. It would be difficult to find an unbeliever among the diversified classes of those who deny the inspiration of the Bible, who is not, at brain and heart, an evolutionist, with some sort of theory that entirely does away with God, or puts him at a distance so remote, so inactive, that he is scarcely to be thought of, much less obeyed and worshipped as a divine and imminent Being.

We think it would be difficult to find a university in this country, or any other, that is not dominated by teachers who are evolutionists; some of them may claim to be theistic evolutionists, but it would be rare to find men of this class who have any sort of established faith or spiritual passion.

The various theories of Evolution, as accepted, believed and taught in textbooks, magazines, newspapers and popular fiction have gone a long way toward the destruction of evangelical Christian faith in all the civilized nations of the world. We cannot condemn the intelligent people of Spain, France, Italy, Mexico and South American countries for their rebellion against the tyrannical government, superstitions and idolatry of Roman Catholicism; but let it be remembered that these peoples, millions of them, who are turning away from Romanism, are not turning to Christ and the Bible for the guide of their lives and the salvation of their souls. They are largely repudiating the Christian religion; they are becoming infidels, socialists, communists, many of them plunging into the dark night of a blasphemous atheism.

Through the centuries of the false teaching and superstitions of Rome, their mental and spiritual life has been plowed, harrowed and carefully prepared for the reception of atheistic seed that will inevitably produce a harvest of revolution and bloodshed. Modern skeptical teaching, so general in the institutions of higher education throughout the world, has had a tendency to lift the floodgates of sin and produce a generation of people who have lost faith in, and reverence for, God; not only so, but respect for womanhood, for fellowmen, for family relationships, for any sort of serious thinking with reference to the future; believing themselves to be animals, they act the part of animals.

Not long since, Dr. T. F. Gulixson, of St. Paul, Minn., President of the Lutheran Theological Seminary, in an address at a Lutheran Educational Conference in Cincinnati, said: "When we elders speak of the revolt of youth and stand in horror at the morals of today, let it be remembered that where young folk live like pagans it is because their fathers, for a generation, have been thinking like pagans. Elders cannot hire teachers by the thousand to teach children that they are beasts, and expect to escape the consequences of beastly living."

Referring to the chapter under the head of "What Our Young People Are Being Taught," we wish to call attention to a perfect flood of the most dangerous sex literature which is deluging the country. It seems strange that a self-respecting, God-fearing

Is the World Growing Worse? 117

government would permit such literature to be carried by the mails, in fact, become a party to the distribution of this salacious stuff by carrying it abroad through the land for the ruin of the home and the moral blight of the youth of the nation.

Recently I picked up in one of the bookstores, a volume by one of the large publishing companies, written by a certain German philosopher. I will not give the name of the book or its author. You will at once get some conception of the attitude and spirit of the writer when I give you the following lines: "The tender-hearted appreciation of companionate marriage wisely sponsored by Ben Lindsey." You see that he has a word of praise for Lindsey and his proposed trial marriages, which simply means to license, dignify and make adultery respectable. He also commends the position of Bertrand Russell and his assault upon the sacredness of the marriage relation.

One of the early statements in the book to which I refer, reads like this:

"Static morality has been repudiated in favor of dynamic experience.

Fear yields its sovereignty reluctantly to fun. Virginity is sacrificed to felicity. Virtue, being its own reward, is bartered away in favor of love. Passion's coming of age heralds the dawn of a new orientation in the life of the sexes. We may sum up the quintessence of sexual revolution by saying the center of gravity has shifted from procreation to recreation."

The writer says all of this, not with regret, but approval of such conditions.

Here is another quotation from this literary sewer:

"To sum up: marriage as conventional coercion is on the verge of bankruptcy. Marital love as ritual and routine is no longer honored as either sacred or sweet. Morality as the sheer perverse tyranny of abstraction is dethroned. Experience as the open sesame of life more abundant is being welcomed as essentially good."

Bear in mind that the author of this book is undertaking to tell of existing con-

Is the World Growing Worse? 119

ditions with full encouragement and endorsement.

In the following quotation the writer gives full vent to the feelings of his "ideal man."

"What few persons as yet clearly perceived is the relation between the contemporary exchanges in morals, and the first beginnings of that scientific revolution three hundred years ago which is responsible for all the changes in the modern world. Man confronted nature insolently and said: I am not to be deterred any longer from inquiring into the deepest mysteries, the most sacred intimacies of your behavior. I have invented a clever method of probing the most underlying truths of your existence. I call that method of trial and error the scientific technique of experimentation. Henceforth nothing shall remain closed and private and too sacred for my piercing and profane investigation. The scientific revolution, skeptic, blasphemous, merciless, is on. Long live the scientific revolution. The sexual revolution is the most recent and the most profound phase of scientific revolution: the drastic application of the principle of experimentalism to life in all its personal aspects. The sexual revolution is inevitable. The mother image fades into obscurity and out of that image of purity emerges the image of the sweetheart as the inspiration of man's life."

The writer goes forward with this sort of declaration:

"Marriage no longer binds. Marriage no longer unites. Marriage as a sacred psycho-sexual union conceived in heaven and perpetuated on earth is no longer meaningful to us. The habit of marriage remains. The psychology of marriage has petered out. The custom of marriage is still with us. The familiar wistful sanctions of marriage are now a chapter in antiquarian lore. The new casual way of sexing has modified all our traditional thinking on the subject of holy matrimony."

I am sure the reader has had enough of

Is the World Growing Worse? 121

this, but we feel it is important that the better class of people should know what is going on in the world, and what is the outcome and fruitage of the teachings being given in many of our institutions of learning. Here is a sample from the book under consideration:

"Family life as such is on the wane. Instability of marital ties is the outstanding fact. Infidelity is no longer deemed a violation of a sacred vow. A kind of loosening of the old erotic bonds is occurring among all strata of the population, among young and old, good and bad, male and female. This loosening of the old erotic bonds is what is technically called, the new morality. The new morality is really new in the original sense that it assigns a status of reasonable reputability to behavior branded throughout the moralistic Christian centuries as immoral, disreputable."

We regret to be compelled to admit that this atheistic philosopher has much truth mixed with his falsehood. There is a fearful drift in this nation, and in the world, away from reverence for any and everything that is true, good and divine. The animal idea that has been promulgated in schools by the teaching of Evolution has gone a long way toward the breaking down of Christian civilization, and destroying one of its chief foundation stones—the sacredness of marriage and the purity of the home, which scriptural marriage secures. The frightful thing about it is that the writer from whom we quote, is rejoicing over the disaster. He is fiddling a jazz tune while Rome burns. He is a bold and defiant advocate of free love. The bloody bloom of atheism at its nth power in Russia, he wears with delight as his buttonhole bouquet.

True, this writer, with all others of his class who delight to bathe and swim in sexual filth is, or would be, a glib liar, but for the fact that he and his associates have lived in a moral realm so low and unclean that they have become blinded to the fact that there is any purity in the world; that there are millions of happy, congenial, decent marriages and homes in which everything

Is the World Growing Worse?

that is best is sought, cultivated and reverenced.

You must bear with me in one more quotation from the book under consideration. I wish to give you a look into the atheistic soul of this advocate of free love, this champion for the desecration of the home and the pollution of womanhood. We quote:

> "The ritual of fear has embodied itself in such noble and soul-destroying conceptions as God, Fate, Death, Immortality, Evil, Confessional, Prayer, Magic. By a myriad subtle devices man has sought to cleanse his human nature of its infinite pettiness and mean inferiority by postulating spiritual sawdust twins, such as the holy virgin or God and Jesus, to scrub away the filth of his morality. The misery of man has resided in his grotesque fear of death and in his even more incredible fear of life. He has projected out these weird infantile fears upon inscrutable powers supposedly at work in the universe for his undoing unless periodically placated."

In former times the atheists and infidels of this country found a degree of satisfaction, sitting in the back rooms of barrooms and, over their social glass of whiskey, tearing the Bible to pieces, blaspheming God and ridiculing Christianity. But there has come a radical change in their attitude; they have marshalled their ever increasing forces and sallied forth from barrooms and bawdy houses and made a bold frontal attack upon everything that is pure and sacred. They have gotten a strong hold on the centers of higher education; they have found an open channel for the propaganda of their destructive teaching through the daily press, the monthly magazines, and popular fiction. They have succeeded in getting much of their skeptical thought into the textbooks of the schools. The highlights and darlings of the moving picture people are saturated, soul and body, with very few exceptions, with the "new morality," which is a modern definition for the old immorality.

These atheistic enemies of God and humanity would do away with the marriage relation, entirely, and have a generation

Is the World Growing Worse? 125

born out of wedlock, and teach them to glory in the fact that they were the products of an impure and indecent parentage. They are striving to bring our American civilization, as well as that of the entire civilized world, to a condition of immorality, lust and libertinism that would shock the lowest tribes of half-naked savages.

The reader must not be deluded with the hope that these men who are so busily engaged sowing tares in the wheat fields of American society, are laboring in vain; they are having marvelous success. Not long since, a friend of mine had several debates on the question of trial marriages with Judge Lindsey. He told me that at the close of these debates, while the older people gathered about him to shake his hand and thank him for the defense of the home, that the young people in the audience flocked about Lindsey with enthusiasm, endorsing his position and thanking him for his illuminating message. This is something to provoke serious reflection.

One of the unfortunate features of the situation is the fact that the preaching and teaching of modern, liberal preachers and teachers are preparing the mental and spiritual soil to receive the seed of most dangerous skeptical and atheistic sowing. These same modernistic preachers and teachers will tell you, with enthusiasm, that the world is growing better.

CHAPTER XII.
THE GENERAL DRIFT.

There are currents of thought among men something like the Gulf Stream in the ocean. There are times when, under their leaders, the masses of the people are powerfully influenced in certain directions. We have had in this nation a very remarkable trend toward the material.

Perhaps there has been no nation in history where everybody was so eager for wealth, as in these United States the past three or four decades. The pioneers of this country worked hard to make an honest living, and sought to protect themselves from marauding bands of Indians. They were kept busy turning the forests into fields, frequently fleeing to their stockades to save their scalps. They were a hardy and virtuous people, and laid the foundation for a splendid civilization.

The progress and development of this country since the close of the Civil War have surpassed anything known in the history of mankind. The development of railroads, building of great cities, the manufacturing interests, the mining of coal, iron, and the more precious metals, along with millions of wealth that has been produced by the discovery of vast lakes of oil beneath the surface of the earth, with the unparalleled development of farming and stock raising, has given to this country a half century of progress and the accumulation of wealth unknown in the annals of history. As one travels from coast to coast, and lakes to Gulf and looks upon the great cities, the beautiful towns, the country dotted over with villages, the vast farms, with their palatial homes, and undertakes to make some estimate of the millions of money realized in this nation in one year from the sale of cotton, wheat, corn, vegetables, citrus fruits, peaches, melons, berries and the various meat products, one is almost appalled at the millions of money that comes to the American people in the short period of twelve months.

It appears that almost everybody has come under the influence of an irresistible desire to become rich; this desire is not confined to any one class of people; the millionaires are eager for more money and common laborers are discontented with anything less than the luxuries of life, with dreams of becoming quite well to do. Farmers, lawyers, politicians, merchants, ministers of the gospel, the show people, real estate men, fakers, people everywhere, have seemed to be in the eager pursuit, not of the necessaries and simple comforts of life, but of wealth.

It is quite safe to say that the general drift in this nation for a number of decades has been decidedly materialistic. Unfortunately, a large per cent of the people have seemed to be indifferent to ethical standards in their eagerness to possess themselves with gold, regardless of the methods used by them to secure their wealth. Money hides a multitude of sins from the eyes of those who are blinded by the desire for wealth. This passion for material possessions has become a fire that has consumed honor, charred honesty, and seared the consciences of multitudes of our American people. The words trust, confidence, integrity, fidelity and covenant have almost lost their meaning.

Not long since, I clipped from that very excellent paper, *The Christian Advocate,* from the clear mind and facile pen of James L. Finney, the following:

> "One of the most disquieting signs of the times is the effort being made in a number of States to bring about prosperity through pandering to the weaknesses, the foibles, and the passions of mankind. In a number of States the Legislatures this year have been engaged in a discreditable rivalry to obtain the so-called profits of easy divorce mills. In other States, suffering from the drought and the financial debacle, suggestions of similar legislation to restore better times are being seriously entertained.
>
> "It is a common delusion with a large element of the population that profit can be derived from vice. We forget the experience of mankind when we insist that we can find economic security by avoiding the paths of virtue or removing the sanctions of conventions. There may be, and doubtless is,

an occasional boom resulting from a letting down of the bars. Those who have more money than morals, who crave excitement and change, will flock to a 'wide-open State' or a community where evil flourishes; but in the end the people suffer, even in an economic sense, more than they ever gain.

"No enduring prosperity can be built upon the insecure foundations of easy divorce, loose morals, gambling, or by otherwise pandering to the vices of man. These things leave a brood of evils in their wake that ultimately cost the community far more than a little temporary prosperity.

"But this false standard is one of the inevitable results of the gross materialism of the age. We have been bowing down and worshipping the god of prosperity until we have an utterly confused sense of values. We measure everything in dollars and cents. We appraise all virtues in terms of their monetary worth."

A few years ago the Reverend Charles E. Jefferson, D.D., pastor of Broadway Tabernacle, New York City, gave the public a very interesting book with the suggestive title, "Five Present-Day Controversies." The book was published by Fleming H. Revell Company. In the five discussions Dr. Jefferson covers much controverted territory. He is a man of scholarship, wide reading and very well posted. From this book we produce a quotation that is quite interesting. It must be understood Dr. Jefferson is not by any means a religious fanatic. He is religious, but is not a radical. He is not an excitable man. The quotation which we give here is from his chapter on Catholicism and the Ku Klux Klan.

"America has been, and still is, in bad shape. It is foolish to say that it is not. Look at the list of murders! No other country under heaven has such a list. Look at the list of burglaries committed not simply in New York City, but in every city of the country. No other nation can show records blacker than that. Look at the list of

Is the World Growing Worse? 133

our lynchings. No other civilized nation has a record so shameful. Look at the list of our strikes. In no other country is the conflict between labor and capital so implacable and so bitter. Look at the list of our scandals—our commercial scandals, and our political scandals. One after another they come, until the heart of the people is made sick. Every few months a new form of rottenness is uncovered. Our corruption 'is rank—it smells to heaven.' And then look at our lawlessness. It is not simply the Volstead Act that is flouted and trampled on, but *all* law. We are becoming more and more, a lawless people.

"And where are we to look for relief? Certainly not to the national Government. There is no balm in *that* Gilead. Our Government is so constructed that a little company of foolish and stubborn men can tie it into a hard knot, so that democracy is incapable of functioning at all. The national government is paralyzed again and again by the spirit of partisanship. We cannot look for help to our political parties. Both of the great political parties are morally bankrupt. What can they do to help us out of our distresses? We cannot go to the courts. Our Secretary of State, Mr. Hughes, said the other day that we make twelve thousand new laws every year in this country. He called attention to the confusion resulting from clashing interpretations and judgments. The processes of our judicature are so technical and complicated, that lawsuits drag on interminably. Many of our leading lawyers have been telling us for years that a poor man stands little chance of getting justice in our courts. A rich man, or a rich corporation can appeal a case from one court to another, until the poor litigant is either in the poorhouse or in his grave. The administration of criminal law has broken down in various parts of the country. Only a few of the criminals are caught, and of those who are caught only a few are convicted, and of the few who are convicted only a small

Is the World Growing Worse? 135

fraction ever serve out their sentence. It seems hopeless to secure justice through the courts. We cannot go to the churches. The churches are numerous and active, but they are unable to focus their moral forces on the spot where it is most needed. We have all sorts of organizations created for numberless good purposes, but all of them stand impotent in the presence of this flood of lawlessness and godlessness which is sweeping across the land."

The learned Doctor gives us a very dark picture, but he has not overdrawn its blackness. We might add some very strong touches of color without exaggeration. At the present moment there are a number of millionaires of this country furnishing the money to enlist all the most dangerous elements of the nation in a gigantic effort to bring back upon the people the liquor traffic, with its waste of the hard-earned wages of the poor, the breaking up of homes, the destruction of the bodies and souls of the people; and one of the amazing features of it all is, these human vultures have lost all sense of shame; they are bold and defiant in their selfish enterprise. They do not hesitate to proclaim abroad that one of their objects is to escape the paying of taxes on their millions of income, and to shift the burden of the government from a comparatively small per cent of their vast millions to drain the pockets of the poor.

There is another reason why these selfish money-lords want to bring back the liquor traffic. King Whiskey has always, when upon the throne, been able to dictate, largely, the political issues of the nation. He has selected the candidates for office, put them into whatever positions he desired them to occupy, and dictated their actions. Nothing could contribute more to the decency, and improvement of the people, the election to office of honorable and patriotic men, who would labor and legislate for the social and moral uplift of the people, than the dethronement and destruction of King Alcohol.

There is another phase of present conditions that must not be overlooked. Not long since, some one sent me some pages

Is the World Growing Worse? 137

torn from "Liberty," one of the most largely circulated magazines of the country. These pages contain an article under the head of, "An Unvarnished Portrait of an American Boy." One is startled as he reads, but not so much surprised. Any one who is acquainted, to any considerable extent, with a large per cent of high school students of today, knows that they are very far from any sort of vital Christian faith. They have not been taught with diligent care what the Christian religion is. Their conception of God is that he is arbitrary and tyrannical. They have had no intelligent training at home, Sunday school or church with reference to the necessity of that vital change of heart and character which our Lord calls the "new birth." The simple fact is, millions of our young people do not believe there is a God to whom they are responsible.

The young man in the article referred to is described by his brother, who says:

> "I have met a good many of his friends, and they are like him. My parents knew a good deal about me. They know nothing about my brother.

They have no conception of what he thinks, knows, or does. They never will have any conception. And since my brother's friends are like him, and since those friends, both boys and girls, come from middle class families in New York, and Boston, and Chicago, and St. Louis, and San Francisco, I feel that he must be typical. It would be a terrible shock to most parents if they could spend forty-eight hours with their son or daughter, and if their presence did not handicap the action of their children."

He goes on to show that his brother, an intelligent, overgrown athlete at seventeen years of age, looks upon the church with all of its teachings, as a fading out mythical joke that cannot possibly continue or have any influence over people. This seventeen year old lad does not believe there is a God, nor does he feel that he needs such a Being. He doesn't believe there is anything like a soul, and says without hesitation or concern, "Death will be the end of me." This lad at seventeen

Is the World Growing Worse? 139

will attend dances where the participants dance in the nude, and thinks such conduct is proper. He has no faith in, or reverence for, women whether married or single. He is an evolutionist. He got here somehow by processes about which he knows little and cares nothing. He is a kind of superior animal. He will live for the gratification of his appetites without responsibility here or hereafter.

This writer finds his brother without patriotism or concern for anything more than to simply exist in the gratification of his animal propensities. The writer suggests, and we believe correctly, that he is almost an exact type of a vast army of young people who are turned out of our high schools every year to go to higher institutions of learning, to be confirmed in their skepticism and utter indifference to the higher ideals and convictions that guide the lives, and control the conduct of those who believe the Bible and expect to render an account to God in final judgment.

Any pastor or evangelist who is interested in the conversion of young people will tell you that there is no class of people more difficult to evangelize than high school and college students, who are under the instruction and domination of teachers who have trained them to believe that they have evolved from a lower animal life, and that the impulses arising in them, to what was once regarded as evil actions, are simply the remaining influences and tendencies of the lower animal from which they have evolved, and are not to be restrained, but will be largely the guide of their actions. The present drift in our nation, and the nations of the world, is not only away from the high moral standards, ethical ideals, and spiritual conceptions and developments taught in the Scriptures, but the strong drift, the vast Gulf Stream of thought that is sweeping through the ocean of humanity is toward infidelity, atheism, moral wreckage, spiritual night and chaos.

We clip the following from a recent issue of *The Atlanta Constitution*:

"A new course at Columbia University required of all undergraduates, teaches that the distinction between

Is the World Growing Worse? 141

legitimate and illegitimate parenthood should be abolished.

" 'Rational considerations suggest,' says the course, 'it would be more economical to extend social approval to responsible parents whether inside or outside the marriage relationship.'

"Moreover, the course in contemporary civilization attacks the modern home and family as inadequate in serving the affectional needs of those who have entered into the relationship.

" 'Its purpose,' said John J. Coss, Moore collegiate professor, who is in charge of the course, 'is orientation. Our course involves the teaching of how men have lived in the past and how they live today.'

"The students are told that there is a need in present-day civilization for new forms of unions to replace those of marriage. The unconventional unions have assumed various forms, according to Miss Ruth Reed, author of the readings, but 'primarily they are designed for those who wish some sexual companionship without the close association and manner of life now urged upon married couples, and they aim to meet the need of those women who wish children without the constant association of a man which modern conventional marriage entails.

" 'The family in its present form is inadequate,' the course points out. 'At every period in the history of matrimonial institutions there have been considerable groups of people who have not conformed to the social dicta. Among these people have been artists, seers and poets who, in the conduct of their personal affairs, have been allowed a measure of freedom which has not been accorded to other groups.'

" 'This desire for more personal liberty is now extending, however, to other groups of business and professional classes. The result has been the formation of new forms of marriage and of unconventional unions between men and women of similar background and tastes, in the hope that these unions may prove more amenable to their human needs.' "

Be it remembered that this sort of free love and licentiousness is to be taught in a university of thirty thousand students. The appalling feature of it is that there is moral paralysis and such spiritual deadness in the nation that it will meet with but little protest. The ship of human civilization is moving toward the rocks. There will be a crash!

CHAPTER XIII.

ECCLESIASTICISM VERSUS EVANGELISM

Our Lord Jesus Christ did not come into the world and die to set up a vast ecclesiasticism; he came, lived, taught, died and rose again to set on foot an intense evangelism. It is reasonable to suppose that if God so loved the world as to give his Son to die for its redemption, he would want the world, at the earliest possible moment, to know of his love and of the redemption he has provided.

It is worthy of note that the Lord Jesus, after his resurrection, before his ascension, gave two great commandments: One was to tarry in Jerusalem for the baptism with the Holy Ghost, that his heralds might be endued with power to carry the message swift of foot and hot of heart; the other was, that they go into all the world and preach the gospel to all nations, to all the peoples. He assured his disciples that false prophets would arise, that many would be deceived, that iniquity would abound, that the love of many would wax cold, and that when this gospel of his salvation should be preached for a witness to all nations, that there would come an end. Doubtless he refers to the end of the Church Age, and the coming in of that kingdom which he taught all of his disciples to pray for.

There is not a hint contained in the ministry of Jesus, or in his commandments before his crucifixion, or after his resurrection, indicating any desire for the building up of a vast ecclesiasticism in the world, claiming him as its author or pretending to have his authority for any such creation. We cannot believe that the building of vast cathedrals costing millions of dollars, while the people who have never heard the gospel are neglected, and those who had heard something which pretended to be the gospel, were heavily taxed to build and support cathedrals, palaces and pompous prelates, has any sort of authority from the teachings of our Lord Jesus; in fact, it is entirely contrary to the whole spirit of the New Testament, and the character, life and words of our blessed Lord while he lived and moved among men.

We are not thinking solely of those vast

cathedrals of Europe that have been shrines for the worship of plaster of Paris images of supposed saints, but we are thinking of the expensive churches being erected in this country by the various Protestant denominations; vast plants that cost hundreds of thousands of dollars for their erection and maintenance, and pastors with a corps of assistants that lay a heavy burden upon the people, where revivals are not held, and the conversion of a soul to Christ never takes place; but all sorts of unscriptural methods are resorted to, to bring people into the church in order to keep up its religious showing, and support its expensive institutions, while the "ye must be born again" of the Lord Jesus is not only ignored, but strenuously opposed.

As ecclesiasticism grows, becomes rich, erects massive churches, plants and institutions, seeks after the rich to support it, and guards against a saving gospel that would rebuke the sins and worldliness of the rich, evangelism disappears. There was a time when Methodism was "Christianity in earnest"; when the preachers were on fire with holy zeal, and the people had the glad testimony of perfect love, and the whole business of the church was to seek and save the lost. But as she has grown in wealth, and become a powerful ecclesiasticism, she quenches her evangelistic fire, opposes revivals of religion, and arrays herself against the doctrines and experiences that once made her the mighty power of God in the world for the salvation of the lost, and a spiritual salt permeating and elevating society.

The rebellion against the Roman Catholic Church in Spain is the uprising of the people against an ecclesiasticism that has given them stones instead of bread, and fed them on scorpions rather than fish. The Spanish people, for centuries, have been burdened with heavy taxes to support a pompous priesthood; they have worn the iron yoke of a dictatorial ecclesiasticism, while their souls have been left to starve for the bread of life, the saving gospel of the Lord Jesus Christ. These deceived and burdened people have arisen in indignation against this ecclesiastical tyranny, have burned churches, driven out priests, and doubtless committed most unseemly outrages, but it is the logical sequence of the burden and tyranny of an ecclesiasticism that has lost and quenched all evangelistic passion, and led the people into the dense darkness of an unbelief and skepticism that now flings a dead church away with contempt.

The same is true with reference to Mexico. These deluded people have groaned under the burden of an expensive, idolatrous ecclesiasticism which has worshipped the priesthood and looked to an infallible Pope for water to refresh their souls, while they have grown weary with waiting and struggling under their burdens, and have risen up in utter disgust and anger against a pompous, dictatorial, ecclesiasticism. No doubt, in many instances the people of Mexico, in their rebellion against Romanism, have been unwise, and have gone to extremes, but what else can be expected after years of religious slavery and spiritual starvation.

Conditions in Russia today are the revolt of the people, not only against the church, but against God; their hatred of the Bible, their seizure of church buildings for amusement halls, museums and centers of blas-

Is the World Growing Worse? 149

phemy has never been equalled in any heathen country. It is, in its wickedness, beyond the most fearful apostasy of ancient Israel. It goes far beyond the horrors of the Dark Ages; but there is a reason: it is the harvest of the sowing of the centuries of an ecclesiasticism that had driven out of its heart and life almost every vestige of the evangelistic spirit. The persecutions of the Greek Catholic Church against any and all people that undertook to maintain and cultivate any sort of spiritual evangelism became desperate almost beyond the power of the human mind to imagine.

As you study history and look at conditions around you, you will find that this has always been the tendency of the Church, when it becomes rich, when it erects vast plants, when it builds up a powerful officialism, when it legislates for its material growth and power rather than its evangelism and spiritual development; when it sets its thought and heart upon the visible, rather than the invisible, the material rather than the spiritual. When it is more concerned to elect and elevate rulers than it is to consecrate and send forth evangelists.

We regret to record, but to be true to current history, we are compelled to say that for several decades Methodism has turned her face toward the building of a great ecclesiasticism, rather than toward a warm-hearted, Spirit-filled evangelism. She is beginning to realize the sad results of this tendency. Many of her leaders, as ecclesiastics have always been, are blind to conditions and deaf to protest. They have their meetings, appoint their committees, and make some sort of empty gestures in seeking after a remedy for the present dearth of spirituality and healthy growth, meanwhile they ignore the Bible doctrines and spiritual experiences that made Methodism a flame of evangelistic fire.

We have reached a period in the life of men when history is made swiftly. Inspired prophecy is being fulfilled more rapidly than ever before. We are making more history in a decade than used to be made in a century. The people of this country will not be satisfied in their religious life to mark time, to pay their money for bait and see no fish caught. There are right now mutterings of rebellion against a modernistic,

Is the World Growing Worse? 151

ecclesiastical leadership that entirely fails to break the bread of life to the hungry multitudes. The mass of the Protestant churches in this country is made up, or else, has been developed from the common people, that class who heard Jesus gladly. They want a religion that saves men from sin in this life. They want a salvation that brings peace and joy. They want a warm-hearted devotion rather than stately deadness. They are willing to give time and money for an earnest evangelism that brings the multitudes of the lost to Christ, but they are unwilling to give moral or financial support to a skeptical, burdensome ecclesiasticism which seeks to quench and trample out of existence an eager, spiritual evangelism.

There is a teaching in our Lord's Sermon on the Mount which seems to have been overlooked, that should claim very special attention at this period in the history of the church life of this nation. For fear the reader has no Bible convenient, we shall quote the saying of our Lord to which we desire to call attention. "Ye are the salt of the earth: but if the salt have lost its savor: wherewith shall it be salted? It is thenceforth good for nothing, but to be cast out, and to be trodden under the foot of men." This saying of Christ in the Sermon on the Mount has not had proper exegesis and consideration. It is understood that Jesus is here, not only speaking to the disciples in his presence, but to his disciples in all time to come. He is saying to his Church, for all the future, until his appearing, "Ye are the salt of the earth." And he is warning his Church that it may lose its savor, its saving power. He is teaching us that when the Church loses its power to save men from sin, it is worthless, that then it is to be cast out as something that is of no further use; not only so, but that it is to be, and will be, trodden under foot of men.

It is worthy of note here, that Jesus taught that an ecclesiasticism which loses its evangelistic spirit will become hated of the men that it fails to save, and that they will trample it under foot. This teaching of our Lord was a prophecy that is now taking place in Russia, in Spain, in Mexico, and will take place in these United States if the ecclesiasticism continues its war against evangelism, and does not awaken to the

Is the World Growing Worse? 153

spiritual dearth and the urgent need of a religious awakening, and a great revival of the lukewarm membership of the sleeping multitudes, and a powerful evangelistic movement kindling holy fires of devotion in the church itself, and winning the lost millions to Christ.

Right now, a bold and defiant atheism, with a rabid and godless communism, is driving the hobnails in the soles of their powerful shoes to trample a spiritless ecclesiasticism under their blasphemous feet. Modern liberalism in pulpits and church schools has been sowing the seed of unbelief in the minds and hearts of the rising generation that has produced, and is producing millions of brilliant skeptics that ought to have been evangelized, reborn and brought into the churches.

Much has been said about revising the Methodist Hymn Book. We append here a pithy paragraph from the celebrated writer, Arthur Brisbane:

> The Methodist Church will discard many of the old Wesley and other hymns, some because they are dull, oth-

ers because they are too full of "imagery of blood."

Charles Wesley, eighteenth child of Samuel Wesley, brother of John Wesley, wrote several thousand hymns.

One rejected, has these two lines:

"The pains, the groans, the dying strife
Fright our approaching souls away."

Another, by Isaac Watts, has this verse:

"To the blest fountain of thy blood
Incarnate God, I fly:
Here let me wash my spotted soul
From crimes of deepest dye."

The Methodists feel that hymns of this kind do not appeal to young people of today. Nevertheless, things will not seem the same with the old hymns gone. At prayer meetings in the old Jackson schoolhouse, of Fanwood, N. J., the small gathering felt that religion was serious, when David Hand, and all his children, joined with Ash-

Is the World Growing Worse? 155

ley Grace, Gracie Beck, Mr. Hall and the others in singing:

"Alas, and did my Saviour bleed, and
    did my Sovereign die?
Would he devote that sacred head for
    such a worm as I?"

Skeptical preachers in their pulpits and unbelieving teachers in church schools have taught so much falsehood to the young people under their influence that they have largely turned away from Bible salvation, and now they raise a hue and cry that the Hymn Book must be revised, and the Blood Atonement so modified that these cultured young skeptics may be induced to get together in their Epworth League meetings and ice cream suppers and parlor dances.

We would call their attention to an earnest warning in the sixth chapter of the Epistle to the Hebrews, which reads as follows: "For it is impossible for those who were once enlightened, and have tasted of the heavenly gift, and were made partakers of the Holy Ghost, and have tasted of the good word of God, and the powers of the world to come, if they shall fall away, to renew them again unto repentance; seeing they crucify unto themselves the Son of God afresh, and put him to an open shame."

We have here a most remarkable description of the new birth, with the powerful witness of the Spirit, and the great danger of the rejection of Jesus by those who have enjoyed this marvelous grace, this gracious experience. To discount the death and atoning blood of Jesus Christ for the forgiveness of sins is to recrucify him. We find that this is a climax sin for which there is no repentance. Christ and him crucified was the major in the gospel message of the great Apostle Paul, and must remain so if we expect salvation. The gaily young people of the churches in their dances, shows, card parties and church pageants and immodest dress will come to a crucified Christ whose blood cleanseth from all sin, or they will die and go into eternal darkness. There isn't a more dangerous set of men on earth, or a set of men that will meet more fearful destruction in the day of judgment, than those apostate preachers who have comforted the deluded young people who are being carried away with false

Is the World Growing Worse? 157

teaching and erroneous notions about the blood atonement Jesus Christ made upon the cross for a lost world.

The time has fully come for that vast multitude of preachers and people in Protestantism who hold steadfastly to the Bible doctrines of the atonement, the importance of repentance, the regeneration of the individual, the sanctifying power of the Holy Spirit, and a consecrated, holy life to rise in righteous indignation against those men, preachers and teachers, who are destroying the spiritual life of the church, and endangering the whole fabric of our civil and social life, as well as the purity and power of the Church.

If Abraham could have found ten righteous souls in those doomed cities, Sodom and Gomorrah would have been spared. We must not lose sight of the fact that there must be some spiritual life in the world, a church which is the genuine Bride of Christ, a spiritual salt that penetrates, purifies and preserves, a divine light among men which illuminates society, in order that we may have a civilization worth while, the suppression of crime, the purifying of society; a spiritual cement that binds together the forces that make for good government, the protection of the home, and decent living.

The need of a revival of Bible salvation is great beyond the power of words to express. The fields are white unto harvest; we are living in perilous times; there is but one remedy—the gospel of the crucified Lamb of God that taketh away the sin of the world. One of the most thoughtful men of the nation, said some years ago, contemplating conditions, "We had come to a crisis when it is Christ or chaos."

World conditions are growing worse. The people are in confusion; they have lost faith in their religious and political leaders; they are afraid to trust their children in the schools of the churches; they are afraid to trust their money for safe keeping in the bank; they hesitate to believe what they hear from the pulpit; they look into the future with a feeling of uncertainty and distress of mind. The nations have become trucebreakers; their covenants are "scraps of paper." There is renewed preparation for war throughout the world; suspicion, jealousy and hatred fill the atmosphere

Is the World Growing Worse? 159

with a denseness that portends a reign of terror of blood and fire unknown in the history of mankind. There is but one remedy, and that remedy is in Jesus Christ. He must be preached, he must be sought, he must be found in saving faith, he must be lifted up by a consecrated, prayer-drenched, blood-washed, Spirit-filled church until men will see him, cast away their sins and doubt, fall at his feet and cry, like one of old, "My Lord and my God!"

CHAPTER XIV.
ARE WE APPROACHING THE END OF THE AGE?

It would be unreasonable to suppose that a God great enough to create a universe, of which our globe is a part, with the intelligent beings upon it, would do so without an objective. It is inconceivable that so great a Being would create so vast a universe, and such beings as ourselves at haphazard, with no definite end in view, no fixed purpose or program to carry on and bring into maturity an objective. The end God has in view is far vaster than we can comprehend; it not only covers all time, but reaches out into eternity. We are quite sure, however, from reading the Scriptures that God's objective embraces divine order on this planet; not only redemption of individuals, but a period of righteousness and peace among men, beyond anything that has yet been attained. The Scriptures plainly promise us a warless world.

The ancient Hebrew prophets blazed a trail of divine revelation through the unknown future that has become the highway over which the nations of the earth

Is the World Growing Worse? 161

have traveled up to the present time, and over which they will move to the end of the ages, culminating at the final judgment day when all men shall render an account of their conduct to God.

The remarkable fulfillment of prophecy furnishes us with positive proof of the divine inspiration of the Holy Scriptures. The prophets saw clearly, and wrote accurately of the coming events of the future, reaching out thousands of years beyond the times in which they lived, events that have been fulfilled with such minuteness and detail that they leave no room to doubt that they were divinely inspired.

The cogs in the wheel of prophecy have fit so accurately into the cogs of the wheel of history, as time has moved forward, that it would seem stupid to doubt that God has foreknown coming events, and has revealed to mankind through his prophets many of the great occurrences in the history of the world.

The student of the prophecies written by Daniel, and those contained in the book of Revelation, it occurs to us, can come to but one conclusion, and that is, that as we approach the end of the present age we may expect a time of great tribulation. St. Paul, in his second Epistle to Timothy, gives a description of perilous times that shall come in the last days, which seems to be remarkably applicable to the times in which we are living. We read: "In the last days perilous times shall come. For men shall be lovers of their own selves, covetous." He might have added that wealthy men would build chain stores, buy up the necessaries of life, drive small merchants out of business, and gather the wealth of the nation into the coffers of the few; however, his expression covers the ground thoroughly without going into detail. "Lovers of their own selves, covetous." We read further, "Boasters, proud, blasphemers, disobedient to parents, unthankful, unholy." This scripture applies forcibly to the great nation of Russia in a most remarkable way. The conditions mentioned are not confined to Russia, but as no other nation in the history of the world has become so blasphemous as has Russia, we refer especially to that country.

In a recent issue of the magazine called "Time," we find the following:

Is the World Growing Worse? 163

"Common in Soviet cartoons is a comical little old man, always accompanied by a comical little white bird. The little old man, who has wings, flops awkwardly about, annoying comrades who sometimes smack him with a fly swatter while the little white bird squawks in terror. The little old man is labelled 'God,' the little white bird 'Holy Ghost,' and both are kept constantly in red cartoons by the zealous efforts of Comrade Emilian Yaroslavasky, leader of the society of the godless."

It would be difficult to imagine anything more blasphemous. I could glean from a number of Christian weeklies published in this country, an attitude toward conditions in Russia so generous, that one would feel the writers and editors of these periodicals did not look with any degree of serious concern upon the stark atheism, opposition to Christian religion, and blasphemy so characteristic in Russia today. I repeat Paul's reference to "disobedient to parents, unthankful and unholy," which shall characterize the last days. It is understood that in Russia parental control is practically in the discard. What about this same startling fact in these United States! There is no one thing better known, which gives cause for greater uneasiness among thoughtful people, than the disappearance of family government in our country.

Paul tells us that in these last days the people shall be "unholy." We can hardly think of anything that will raise greater protest in the average Protestant Church than that a minister of the gospel should stand up in the pulpit Sabbath morning and declare that God requires holiness, that is, freedom from sin; that he provides for it in the atonement, and will demand it at the judgment bar. Preaching of this character will arouse the bitterest prejudice and almost unanimous protest. A very large per cent of the Protestant ministers of these United States, at this time, are devoting much of their energy to an almost bitter and vehement denial of the possibility of any one being holy, that is, being saved from all sin in this life.

The Apostle goes on to say that the people in these last days will be "without natural affection, trucebreakers, false accusers, incontinent, fierce, despisers of those that are good." The Apostle was a prophet; he was a *fore*teller as well as a *forth*teller. He was, perhaps, looking into this age of birth control, of not only the preventing of conception, but the destruction of the unborn, and the adoption of dogs, monkeys and cats by women of wealth and leisure, thus turning natural affection out of its course and pouring their love upon animals instead of babes.

Reading on, we find the Apostle telling us that in these last days people will be "traitors, heady, highminded, lovers of pleasure more than lovers of God; having a form of godliness but denying the power thereof." It is interesting to note that the class of persons described in this prophecy of the Apostle, with reference to the last days, are church members; that they make a profession of religion; they "have a form of godliness but deny the power thereof." They ignore the person and offices of the Holy Spirit. They ridicule everything that is supernatural. They love the pleasures of the world; they have religious forms and ceremonies, which they substitute for the atoning merit of Christ and the gracious work of the Holy Spirit in the regeneration and sanctification of human souls.

We can but believe that the thoughtful reader will agree with us that the description St. Paul gives here, in the third chapter of the Second Epistle to Timothy, is a very graphic pen picture of much that exists in the church today. We doubt if there has been a time in the history of mankind upon this globe when there has been such uncertainty, unrest, loss of confidence and a widespread spirit of hatred, godlessness and blasphemy as there is at the present time.

There is no promise in the teachings of Christ that this world will be brought into a gracious state of peace, tranquillity and harmonious union among its peoples prior to his coming; exactly the reverse is taught. Take the sayings of the Lord in the 21st chapter of St. Luke's gospel: "Upon the earth distress of nations, with perplexity; the sea and the waves roaring; men's hearts failing them for fear, and for looking after those things which are coming upon the

Is the World Growing Worse? 167

earth: for the powers of heaven shall be shaken. And then shall we see the Son of man coming in a cloud with power and great glory. And when these things begin to come to pass, then look up, and lift up your heads; for your redemption draweth nigh. And he spake to them a parable; behold the figtree, and all the trees; when they shoot forth, ye see and know of your own selves that summer is now nigh at hand. So likewise ye, when ye see these things come to pass, know ye that the kingdom of God is nigh at hand."

The Lord Jesus goes on to show us that the world will not be expecting his appearing at the time of his glorious coming. He says: "For as a snare shall it come on all them that dwell on the face of the whole earth. Watch ye therefore, and pray always, that ye may be accounted worthy to escape all these things that shall come to pass, and to stand before the Son of man."

It is very evident that the conditions indicating his coming, which are as the buds upon the figtree indicating summer, are to be "distress of nations, with perplexity . . . men's hearts failing them for fear, and for looking after those things which are coming on the earth." It is scarcely worth while to suggest to the reader that the conditions foretold by our Lord are among us on every hand. The perplexity existing among men is indicated by the fact that a group of men in these United States evidently believe that, while millions are suffering for bread, we can solve this difficult problem of human starvation by converting grain into beer instead of bread, making the people drunk instead of contented and happy, and in this way bring back prosperity to the nation. Could anything suggest more forcibly the perplexity and ignorance of men; men who are entirely ignorant of God's plan for world redemption.

We are aware that the whole subject of the coming of our Lord is a matter of profane ridicule among skeptics and atheists. It also provokes very strong opposition among many churchmembers, especially among those ministers known as "Modernistic Liberalists." St. Peter, in his Second Epistle, gives a satisfactory answer to this large element of those who bitterly oppose everything that is said with reference to the

Is the World Growing Worse? 169

coming of the Lord Jesus. We read: "But there were false prophets among the people, even as there shall be false teachers among you, who privily shall bring in damnable heresies, even denying the Lord that bought them, and bring upon themselves swift destruction. And many shall follow their pernicious ways; by reason of whom the way of truth shall be evil spoken of. And through covetousness shall they with feigned words make merchandise of you . . . . Knowing this first, that there shall come in the last days scoffers, walking after their own lusts, and saying, where is the promise of his coming? For since the fathers fell asleep, all things continue as they were from the beginning of creation. For this they willingly are ignorant of, that by the word of God the heavens were of old, and the earth standing out of the water and in the water; whereby the world that then was, being overflowed with water perished."

How accurately Peter describes conditions that exist today; false prophets everywhere teaching the people that making a profession of faith in Christ, they can live lives of sin, die in peace and go to heaven.

Mark you, many of the teachers of this fearful heresy are the champions of fundamentalism. On every hand, we have false prophets, preachers in the big pulpits, denying the deity of our Lord, discarding his redemptive sufferings and substituting education and culture for regeneration and sanctification. It is not to be forgotten that they are making merchandise of the people, getting every dollar and dime possible from them, as if by mere money, they could buy redemption for society. They are overlooking individual salvation and talking of social uplift, mass redemption. Nothing can quite stir the excitement and anger of your average ecclesiastic like a sermon or testimony with reference to the coming and glory of the Lord Jesus Christ.

No sound argument for the moral and spiritual improvement of the world can be based upon modern scientific discovery, or upon the vast accumulation of wealth through these discoveries of the comparatively few, and the impoverishment of countless millions. No sort of confidence in the immediate future of peace can be based upon the action of the League of Na-

Is the World Growing Worse? 171

tions or the Disarmament Conference. It will be with a stretch of imagination that any one can insist that in the spiritual life of the Church, the sanctity of the home, the modesty and virtue of womanhood, the cleanness and integrity of manhood, the harmony and good will among nations, that the world is growing better. Those who are of the opinion that world conditions for several decades have grown worse, and that the present outlook does not promise a change for the better, have many sound reasons upon which to base their beliefs.

Those serious people who believe that we are approaching the perilous times which shall immediately precede the appearing of our Lord, have abundant prophecy and teaching in the Holy Scriptures, and world conditions about us everywhere, upon which to base their beliefs. It will be well for all devout people to give careful heed to the word of God, to study the signs of the times, and above all, to keep their wedding garments of righteousness and true holiness unspotted from the world, and the lamp of their spiritual hope well oiled, trimmed and burning.

We know from the inspired prophets, the writings of the apostles, and from the promises of our Lord himself, that Jesus Christ is coming back to this world in majesty and power; that out of the confusion and strife, blood and fire, he will bring order and peace, and set up a reign of righteousness; that he himself will be the supreme Ruler of a world into which he has brought divine order, and a thousand years of peace and good will among men.

THE END

www.ingramcontent.com/pod-product-compliance
Lightning Source LLC
Chambersburg PA
CBHW031353040426
42444CB00005B/280